— PEOPLE TO KNOW —

MALCOLM X

A Voice for Black America

Arthur Diamond

ENSLOW PUBLISHERS, INC.

Bloy St. and Ramsey Ave.   P.O. Box 38
Box 777   Aldershot
Hillside, N.J. 07205   Hants GU12 6BP
U.S.A.   U.K.

For Irina

Library of Congress Cataloging-in-Publication Data

Diamond, Arthur.
    Malcolm X: a voice for Black America / Arthur Diamond.
        p. cm. — (People to know)
    Includes bibliographical references (p.) and index.
    Summary: Describes the life of the controversial African-American
civil rights activist from his troubled childhood, through his years
as a national leader in the Nation of Islam, to his assassination.
    ISBN 0-89490-435-3
    1. X, Malcolm, 1925–1965—Juvenile literature. 2. Black Muslims—
Biography—Juvenile literature. 3. Afro-Americans—Biography—
Juvenile literature. [1. X, Malcolm, 1925–1965. 2. Afro-
Americans—Biography.] I. Title. II. Series.
BP223.Z8L573335 1994
320.5'4'092—dc20
[B]   93-8431
                                              CIP
                                              AC
Printed in the United States of America

10 9 8 7 6 5 4 3 2 1

Illustration Credits:
The Bettmann Archive, pp. 81, 97, 106; Dr. Laurance G. Henry, p. 102; Museum of the City of New York, pp. 28, 30; Paula Wright / Museum of the City of New York, p. 15; Richard Saunders, courtesy of the Schomburg Center for Research in Black Culture, p. 115; © Robert L. Haggins, pp. 9, 61, 76, 87; The Schomburg Center for Research in Black Culture, pp. 13, 17, 23, 46, 53, 99.

Cover Illustration:
© Robert L. Haggins

Contents

Acknowledgements

Thanks to photographer Robert Haggins, authors Bruce Perry and Michael Friedly, and Andrew Jackson, head librarian of the Langston Hughes Branch of the New York Public Library, for their contributions to this book. Of generous assistance, too, were Jim Huffman of the Schomburg Center for Research in Black Culture and Dr. Russell Adams of Howard University. I would like to extend particular thanks to my editor, Damian Palisi, for her expertise and encouragement. And I am most indebted to Irina, Ben, and Jessica, for patience and joy.

1

"Too Much Power for One Man to Have"

One cold evening in the spring of 1957 in Harlem, in New York City, about fifty black men assembled in a street outside a neighborhood police station. The men wore similar dark suits and bow ties and stood at attention, side by side and one behind the other. These men were called the "Fruit of Islam"—the male members of Harlem's Nation of Islam Temple Number Seven. They were awaiting instructions from their leader, now arriving on the scene.

Malcolm X strode to the front of the column of men. Standing an angular six-foot-four, he wore black eyeglasses and an expression of intensity. He would later be described by author and critic Robert Penn Warren as having "dull yellowish skin, pale enough to freckle, pale eyes, hair reddish-coppery."[1]

Malcolm X looked upon his men. In their faces was the discipline and self-respect that had been missing in his own life only a few short years ago, when he had been a petty criminal and street hustler. This was before he had landed in jail, discovered Islam, and changed his name from Malcolm Little to Malcolm X—the X standing for his true name, which he did not know, and replacing the surname given his family by "white oppressors" generations ago.

The New York City police knew about Malcolm X. They knew he had learned about Islam from the teachings of the Nation of Islam, a militant sect made up solely of black Muslims who opposed integration and demanded separation from white society. The police knew, also, that after his release from prison he had founded Muslim temples in several cities and had been steadily organizing and preaching in Harlem for several years now. What the police could not know, though, was the fact that on this night Malcolm X and his Fruit of Islam would grab the attention of an entire city.

Malcolm X ordered his men to remain calm and disciplined and to follow his directions. He then turned and strode up the steps and into the police station. He demanded, as minister of Temple Number Seven, to see Johnson Hinton, a member of the temple. A police official announced that this individual was not on the premises.

The Black Muslim leader had reason to believe that

this was not true. Less than an hour earlier, he had received word that Hinton, a bystander at a street fight between two black men, had refused police orders to leave the scene of the disturbance: Hinton stated that he wanted to make sure that the two men were not beaten by the police. The police were angered by Hinton's refusal and turned on him, beating him with their nightsticks and then shoving him into their squad car. Malcolm X had been notified that Hinton had been taken to this particular police station.[2]

Malcolm X did not accept the official's claim of ignorance about Hinton's whereabouts. The police relented and admitted that the man was there, but they also declared that Malcolm X could not see him. Malcolm X recalls that he had a clear response to this: "I said that until he was seen, and we were sure he received proper medical attention, the Muslims would remain where they were."[3]

Outside the police station, the crowd around the Fruit of Islam had surged to over 2,000. While the police grew more nervous by the minute, the crowd grew more excited. They had not seen any kind of effective, organized confrontation against the police in recent memory.

Finally, the police relented and ushered Malcolm X to a back room where the beaten man was being held in a tiny cell. Malcolm X could hardly contain himself: "He was only semi-conscious," he would later recall. "Blood had bathed his head and face and shoulders."[4] The Muslim leader, quaking with rage, insisted that Hinton belonged in a hospital. Somebody called an ambulance.

After the ambulance arrived and Hinton was carried into it, its driver sped towards nearby Harlem Hospital—with the Muslims and the crowd following behind them, straight up busy Lenox Avenue. Pedestrians stopped to stare at the crowd marching up the street. Men and women emerged from shops, restaurants, and bars. Apartment dwellers came to their windows to gaze in amazement. Many more people joined the march.

At the hospital, as the noisy, angry crowd assembled behind the Muslims, a police official approached Malcolm X. The official abruptly ordered the black leader to make the crowd disperse. With calm assurance, Malcolm X replied that he would wait to hear that Johnson Hinton was receiving good medical treatment, but until that time he would not move. His men, he claimed, were well-disciplined and causing no harm. When the official pointed out the hostility of the crowd behind the Muslims, Malcolm X had an answer ready: "I politely told him those others were his problem."[5]

After a short while the word came from the doctors: while Hinton had suffered a bad head injury (so bad that a steel plate would be implanted in his skull), he was getting the very best of care.

The black man with "too much power": Malcolm X, flanked by bodyguards, on a New York City Street.

That was good enough for Malcolm X. He turned to the Muslims standing patiently in formation. Their eyes were glued to him. The crowd looked on in anticipation. Malcolm X then made a simple gesture with his hand, and the column of Muslims began to disperse. "I gave the order and the Muslims slipped away," he would later remember.[6] While the bystanders around the departing Muslims were noisy and agitated, they, too, soon left the scene. Mark Davies, in his book *Malcolm X: Another Side of the Movement*, reports that a white policeman was heard to say: "This is too much power for one man to have."[7]

Changes came in the wake of this tense evening in Harlem. Johnson Hinton would take legal action against the New York Police Department and wind up winning the largest police brutality judgment ever paid by New York City. The police would certainly update their files on Malcolm X and the Nation of Islam. And most important to Malcolm X was that he and his men were now known throughout Harlem: ". . . the *Amsterdam News* made the whole story headline news, and for the first time the black man, woman, and child in the streets was discussing 'those Muslims.' "[8]

Burning Houses, Broken Homes

One of Malcolm X's earliest memories was of fire and destruction. He would always remember "being snatched awake one night with a lot of screaming going on because our home was afire."[1] The fire was said to have been set by white supremacists. Standing outside in the rural darkness, his siblings and parents beside him, young Malcolm watched helplessly as the house burned to the ground.

Malcolm's father, Earl Little, found another house for his family, as he had several times before and after Malcolm's birth in Omaha, Nebraska, on May 19, 1925. Earl Little was a Baptist preacher with radical ideas, and he wanted to spread those ideas to as many blacks as he could. White neighbors who knew of Earl's ideas always wished for Earl and his family to keep moving on, too.

Earl Little preached the ideas of a black nationalist leader named Marcus Garvey. Garvey, born in Jamaica, had become famous in America in the early part of the century for declaring the need for a black state. The state would be in Africa, at that time almost completely controlled by white governments. In the new state, blacks would be entirely self-sufficient. They would have their own government; would run their own schools; and man their own post offices—just like the people of any nation. There would be no need for any kind of dependence on the American white man, who had captured and enslaved blacks until the Civil War.

Though the Civil War had ended slavery, it could not end racism, and blacks like Marcus Garvey who spoke up too loudly in America were put down. Black leaders feared being attacked and beaten in their churches and homes by white supremacists like the Ku Klux Klan. They feared being shot in the back or hanged from trees. Blacks did not even have to commit the crime of speaking out to be punished—sometimes they were targets merely because of the color of their skin.

Garvey himself was arrested in 1925 by the federal government on charges of using the mails to defraud, and deported to Jamaica two years later, but Earl Little persisted in speaking out. He continued to attend meetings and organize chapters of Garvey's Universal Negro Improvement Association (UNIA) in small Midwestern towns as he moved his family along with

A lynched black man. While the Civil War put an end to slavery, it could not end racism, and blacks throughout the United States and especially in the South were aware that they or their loved ones could be randomly shot in the back or hanged from a tree.

him. He often brought his youngest son Malcolm to the meetings.

While declaring the need for unity and self-sufficiency among blacks, Earl Little did not practice what he preached. According to author Bruce Perry's book *Malcolm: The Life of a Man Who Changed Black America*, Earl Little could not be relied upon to put food on the family table, would fly into a rage and beat his wife and children, and had a reputation for chasing women.[2]

In the East Lansing, Michigan, house where Malcolm spent his boyhood, there was almost always tension between Earl and his wife, Louise. Whereas Earl Little had only a primary school education, Louise Little, raised on the Caribbean island of Grenada, had gone to high school and spoke better English than most of her white neighbors in East Lansing. She often made fun of her husband for what she considered his ignorance.[3]

Both Louise and Earl had mixed feelings about skin color, and this added to the tension in the household. Louise, who was light-skinned, sometimes attacked Malcolm's light skin with a scrub brush to try to make it even lighter. Other times, though, she angrily sent him outside to get more sun and become darker, like his father and the other children.[4] Sometimes she would come after Malcolm and beat him.[5]

Because of Malcolm's light skin, Earl favored him over the other children. Malcolm would escape the

A young boy ponders an alluring advertisement. In the Little household, Malcolm's mother and father often unleashed their anger and frustration upon their children over the explosive issue of skin color.

beatings Louise and the other children suffered from Earl, and Earl would show him off to the white neighbors. Yet, as a Garveyite, Earl Little defiantly denounced the white race to his followers.

On September 28, 1931, Earl Little's defiant voice was silenced forever. According to author Bruce Perry, that night, six-year-old Malcolm and his siblings were roused from sleep first by a knock at the door and then by their mother's horrified screams. Police had come to notify her that Earl Little had been run over in a streetcar accident in Lansing. His left arm had been crushed and his left leg nearly severed. Though Earl Little clung to life until he reached the operating room, the doctors were unable to save him.[6]

Louise Little was determined to provide her children with a good memory of their father. This, she thought, would give them pride and help them through hard times. She told Malcolm and the others what a great and courageous man he was, and how so many people loved and respected him. She didn't talk about his fits of rage and violence, his failings as a provider, or how he was unfaithful to her. The line between fact and fiction must certainly have become blurred for Malcolm and his siblings.

After Earl's death, family, friends, and neighbors tried to be helpful. They came to visit and would help around the house. They helped advise Louise about some money from a life insurance policy Earl left.

A Harlem rally for the UNIA. In the early years of this century many African Americans, including Malcolm's father, Earl Little, joined Marcus Garvey's Universal Negro Improvement Association.

But Earl Little, with all his faults, had been the rule-giver, ultimate authority, and protector of the Little family, and after his death, the family began to come undone. Soon the insurance money was depleted, and there was no more source of income. Friends and neighbors came to help but were shooed away by Louise, who proudly declared she needed no help. She began driving into Lansing to work as a seamstress and a housekeeper, but she would return crying after a few days at a job, having been fired because her employer found out who her husband had been. Malcolm's oldest brother Wilfred dropped out of school and took odd jobs. Malcolm and his younger siblings stayed at home and were supervised by their older sister Hilda, who struggled to maintain the house amid the turmoil left by their mother's absence.

In the early thirties, the Great Depression's economic turmoil affected people's lives all across the country. Americans were hurt and confused as they lost their jobs, watched their savings shrink, and felt the accompanying pressures crowding in on them and their families.

In 1931, young Malcolm felt these economic pressures all around him, as well as the absence of his mother, gone to work, and the absence of his father, gone forever. But like most six-year-olds, he did not talk of his feelings of hurt and confusion; he could not really explain them. He simply absorbed them, and his behavior grew inward and complex.

When it came to fighting, for example, young Malcolm had a strong fear of being hurt. Perhaps this came from being beaten by his mother and also watching his father strike his mother and his brothers and sisters. At school and at the playground, other children sensed Malcolm's fear and called him a coward.[7] When someone bigger than him challenged him, he would become wild and curse and yell insults, and this would usually scare away the aggressor. But sometimes the tactic backfired, and he would suffer a beating from an enraged adversary.

Yet he could overcome his fear and show his courage. According to author Bruce Perry, one day a partly disabled boy riding a bike was bullied into a ditch by some older children of the neighborhood. Malcolm quickly ran over and stood up to the bigger boys and made them leave the smaller child alone.[8]

While young Malcolm struggled with his fears, his family slipped deeper and deeper into poverty. Seasons passed with no hopes for change. In summer the Little children went barefoot and in winter they suffered from the cold. They often ate dandelion greens for dinner. Government workers came to the house with welfare checks and offered to arrange for clothing and new housing for the family, but all such offers were refused.

Although Louise had begun to suffer from mental illness, she still maintained she would take care of her family.

By the fall of 1938, however, living conditions had become even worse for the Littles and Louise gave up on her hope of keeping her family together. In October thirteen-year-old Malcolm got expelled from the Pleasant Grove School for his bad behavior and Louise agreed to allow him to continue school in another Lansing neighborhood. He was sent off to live with an older white couple, Mabel and Thornton Gohanna, who received a fee from the state for boarding troubled children like Malcolm. The other Little children—Wilfred, Philbert, Reginald, Hilda, Yvonne, and baby Butch—were also shuttled off to foster homes.

While living with the Gohannas, Malcolm displayed his talent with words. He did well in his classes at West Junior High School. He excelled in a group discussion program for underprivileged youngsters that was held after school at a local community center. Author Bruce Perry reports that "He was rarely at a loss for words on these occasions . . . it was nearly impossible to silence him once he got the floor. . . . If his authority was questioned, he grew angry."[9]

But he was unsure about the Gohannas. He liked them well enough, but he was not certain they liked him. They treated him well, yet he felt uncomfortable because they were deeply religious people. Living with the Gohannas gave him regular meals and a secure roof over his head, yet he risked it all by continuing his habit of stealing from local stores.

On January 9, 1939, after years of poverty, humiliation, and despair, Louise Little suffered a complete nervous breakdown. She was declared insane by the State of Michigan and was formally committed to the State Mental Hospital at Kalamazoo. She would remain there for the next twenty-six years.

Malcolm barely managed to complete the seventh grade. During the summer, he left the Gohannas and returned to the parentless house in Lansing, where older siblings Wilfred and Hilda tried to keep the family together. Malcolm did not want to stay. He told a visiting social worker that he wished to be sent to a juvenile home. In the fall of 1939, he went to live with Lois Swerlein and her husband in Mason, a small town ten miles south of Lansing.

Malcolm liked Lois Swerlein. He worked part-time for her, and he also worked hard at Mason Junior High School. In fact, he did so well that he ended up ranking third in the eighth grade class at one point. He continued to impress others with his speaking abilities and his courage: according to author Bruce Perry, one winter day Malcolm protected another boy from a gang wanting to place the youngster in an outdoor water fountain.[10]

But there were things about living in Mason that made him feel unwanted. While the Swerleins seemed to be genuinely warm towards him, they also called him a "nigger." Bruce Perry reports that while Malcolm was popular in school and tried to make friends, whites "accidentally" elbowed him in hallways; if there was anything missing at school, he was the first to be blamed.[11]

If feeling unwanted at the Swerleins' and at school had dealt him sharp blows, the knockout punch was delivered by Malcolm's English teacher. One day in the spring of 1939, Malcolm had a talk with Richard Kaminska, a large ex-football player, well-liked by most of his students. Malcolm was asked by Kaminska what his plans were for the future. Malcolm declared that he would like to be a lawyer.

Kaminska's response was not what Malcolm had hoped for. As documented by author Bruce Perry, Kaminska responded, "We all here like you, you know that. But you've got to be realistic about being a nigger. A lawyer—that's no realistic goal for a nigger. You need to think about something you *can* be. You're good with your hands . . . Why don't you plan on carpentry?"[12]

After that encounter, Malcolm no longer paid attention in class. He disrupted school events and got himself kicked out of school on several occasions. He plodded through the rest of eighth grade. Later he would admit, "I just gave up."[13] He longed for a way out of dismal Lansing, and found a way in the person of his

Malcolm as he looked as a teenager.

older half-sister Ella, who lived in Boston, Massachusetts.

Ella Collins, one of Earl Little's three children by a previous marriage, had welcomed Malcolm to Boston in the summer of 1940. During that visit, he was impressed by Ella's confidence and authority. "She was the first really proud black woman I had ever met. I was totally overwhelmed by her."[14] He was also impressed with Boston's big-city life.

In 1941, Ella invited him to come live with her in Boston. He gladly accepted. He had just turned sixteen and had completed the eighth grade. Unloved and unwanted in Lansing, his self-esteem badly damaged, he went east, to Boston, to try life in the big city.

Descent

Ella Collins was a strong-willed person. She had moved to Boston and married a doctor, and though divorced when Malcolm came to stay with her, she was still one of the more respected members of the prominent black neighborhood of Sugar Hill. Sugar Hill was on the border of Roxbury, Boston's black ghetto. Ella wanted good things for Malcolm. She wanted him to be like the people of the Hill.

Malcolm did not like the people of the Hill. He found that when a woman from the Hill claimed she "came from a wealthy family," the truth was she worked as a servant for a rich white person. When a Hill man claimed to be "in banking," he was actually a janitor in a white man's bank. Malcolm was infuriated by what he saw as hypocrisy and self-deception among this better class of blacks.

Malcolm spent his first weeks in Boston down off the Hill, in Roxbury, and the ghetto lit a fire inside him. Here, he felt accepted. He felt a sense of belonging. Back in Lansing, a lone black felt unique, isolated, trapped. In Roxbury, a black could rejoice in the simple pleasure of being among his own people.

While wandering wide-eyed through the busy streets, Malcolm was initially attracted to the pool halls. He observed from the outside what went on inside: youths and men in smoke-filled rooms, calm and confident, relaxing in one another's company, shooting pool, spending time. With some hesitation, he finally stepped inside and met a young man named Shorty, who worked racking up balls for the pool players.

Shorty turned out to be from Lansing, too. He and Malcolm became fast friends. Within a few days, Shorty found him a job as a shoeshine boy at a local dance hall. Though Ella was displeased with the work, she knew, from Malcolm's enthusiasm, that to try to talk him out of it would be futile.

The Roseland State Ballroom was one of Roxbury's prominent nightspots. There was a great waxed floor for dancing and a stage at one end of the hall for the band. At night it was a crowded space, filled with cigarette smoke and warm with body heat. Music from the popular bands of the time, like the Benny Goodman

Band and the Erskine Hawkins Band, floated out the ballroom doors and up to the second-floor restrooms, outside of which Malcolm worked his shoeshine rag on the shoes of the sweaty dancers.

As a shoeshine boy, he learned how to earn a good tip: apply the polish, shine the shoes, snap the towel—customers liked that—and run a whisk broom over their pants and suit. He also learned to make tips by selling condoms and sticks of marijuana out of his coat pocket. These items were in great demand. The greatest demand, however, was for flesh, and he began acting as matchmaker between the races. Black men seeking white women—and vice-versa—gratefully paid for slips of paper with special phone numbers on them.

Malcolm began transforming himself. Desiring to take on the look of the wild dancers he admired, he bought a purple zoot suit. A zoot suit featured pants that flared wildly at the knees and tapered in at the ankles, perfect for dancers who needed freedom of movement. Malcolm also had his hair "conked." Shorty applied a mixture of lye, eggs, and potatoes, which made Malcolm scream. But when the mixture was washed off, Malcolm's reddish hair was straight—just like a white man's.

The next step in Malcolm's transformation was to become a dancer. Tall and rather clumsy, Malcolm worked hard in front of a mirror and in time became one of the better lindy-hoppers at Roseland. Crowds would

While living in Boston, Malcolm worked as a shoeshine boy at a dance hall such as this.

gather around him and his partner as they thrilled the other dancers with jumps, shouts, and thrilling spins. He soon quit his job as a shoeshine boy and spent as much time as he could on the dance floor, enjoying the cheers and applause of other dancers.

Having a good partner to dance with was important. One partner was Laura, an intelligent girl who lived near the Townsend Drugstore, where Malcolm had reluctantly accepted a job as a soda jerk. Laura lived with her strict grandmother and came into the drugstore for banana splits. She soon grew infatuated with Malcolm and began lying to her grandmother so she could stay out late with him dancing. But one night at Roseland, when an attractive white woman named Bea took an interest in Malcolm, Laura was rudely brushed aside. For Malcolm, having a white woman to show off was much more important than keeping a good dance partner—or not hurting her feelings. He was too busy seeking status for himself to care.

When Japan bombed Pearl Harbor on December 7, 1941, America immediately prepared for war; Malcolm only cared about getting to see Harlem. He had always heard of Harlem, New York's famous black community. And one way to get there was having a railroad job, easy to find now that working men all over the country were being drafted into the armed forces. Though well under the required age of twenty-one, Malcolm looked older and had no trouble finding employment.

Malcolm listened and danced to the popular Erskine Hawkins Band
(shown here) during the early 1940s.

He had slacked off in school since being discouraged from a professional career by his English teacher; now, out of school, he showed his ability to work hard. His first job was washing dishes on a train that ran from Boston to Washington, D.C. He loved traveling from city to city on the train and worked so hard to keep his job that fellow workers grew angry, for he made them look lazy by his example. His next job was as a food seller on the train that ran from Boston to New York. He continued to work harder and faster than the others to make sure he kept his job and to earn large tips from the passengers.

Malcolm also displayed his wit and inventiveness. One day, while selling food in the train's crowded dining car, Malcolm was challenged by a drunken soldier to fight. At this time soldiers were common on the trains, and drinking was their usual way to relax. Malcolm, however, could not relax with the soldier threatening to punch him in the face.

The soldier advanced, and Malcolm agreed to fight him—but only if the soldier took his coat off. The soldier promptly removed his coat and stepped toward Malcolm again, but Malcolm stopped him by telling him he'd only fight if the soldier removed his tie. Then came the shirt. In a few minutes, the drunken soldier, half-naked and embarrassed, had been silenced by the clever young waiter. The other passengers roared their approval. Malcolm, the victor, had once again escaped danger by using his mouth.

But he could not escape the overwhelming evidence that he and his people were doomed to live as second-class citizens. Staying over in Washington, D.C., he was revolted by the poverty of blacks living just blocks from Capitol Hill and the White House. Someone explained to him that there were better off middle-class blacks, too—a solid and established community with prestigious jobs. But these prestigious jobs, as Malcolm soon learned, were as mail carrier and cook and taxi driver. It was the same situation as on the Hill back in Boston. Blacks couldn't make it in the white man's world.

But they could "make it" in Harlem. If Boston had been an eye-opener for Malcolm, Harlem was a revelation. From his very first night there, while on a layover from his train job, he was delighted with what writer Roi Ottley called "a vibrant, bristling black metropolis."[1] The music of jukeboxes and calls from street vendors filled his ears, and he breathed in the smells of fish cakes and sweet potatoes mixed with the dank mustiness of shabby hallways. Lovers and strollers shared the sidewalks with streetwalkers and hustlers—and they were all black, all bustling about what Ottley called "the nerve center of advancing Black America."[2]

In Harlem, he would receive an education. One of

his first evenings in Harlem, Malcolm wandered into a bar called Small's Paradise. People in Boston had told him he had to see it. Around the big circular bar sat and stood thirty or forty well-dressed black men in conservative suits and ties and hats. They were Harlem's pimps and hustlers, and they were counting their money, going over accounts, engaging in easy conversation, having a drink. They stopped to eye the young stranger, then assuredly went on with their business.

Malcolm was impressed. He knew he could learn a lot from listening to and working with these "cool characters." He could not know, however, that he was on his way to becoming, in his own words, "one of the most depraved parasitical hustlers among New York's eight million people."[3]

His first big break in Harlem came in the form of a job as a waiter at Small's Paradise. At Small's, he was quickly exposed to ordinary working men, musicians, and hustlers from the Harlem world of crime. He preferred the musicians and hustlers.

As a waiter, he dutifully lit cigarettes and memorized favorite drinks, and he kept his ears open. He received quite an education. The hustlers at Small's shared with him their various secrets—like how to pickpocket or break into an apartment. He learned to supplement his income by arranging meetings between black men and white women, or white men and black women, as he had done as a shoeshine boy back in Boston.

He finally lost his job at Small's after arranging for a prostitute for one customer who turned out to be an undercover policeman. The police knew Malcolm was "small-time," though, and they let him go.

Soon enough, Malcolm had a new job: selling marijuana. He began to make a lot of money at it. With marijuana within reach all the time now, his consumption of it steadily increased. He began peddling cocaine and heroin, too, mostly to local musicians he'd met at Small's. He indulged in those drugs, too, and stayed high on drugs practically all the time. Years later, he would angrily contend that many in Harlem stayed high on dope to "forget what they had to *do* to survive."[4]

His own survival became a game of cat and mouse. The police were onto him and followed him wherever he went, and they often searched and harassed him. Other drug dealers would not mind at all if he just disappeared—and they did not care *how* he disappeared, either. Malcolm understood. He wisely left Harlem and stayed away for awhile, using an old railroad I.D. card to board trains traveling up and down the East Coast, where he sold drugs to musicians traveling from gig to gig.

When he returned to Harlem he had gained the nickname of Detroit Red. At least two other "Reds" were known in Harlem. One, St. Louis Red, was a bank robber. The other, Chicago Red, was a dishwasher Malcolm once worked with in a restaurant. Chicago

Red, according to Malcolm, was the funniest dishwasher alive. Years later, Chicago Red would become famous as comedian Redd Foxx.

Malcolm provided some comic relief of his own when called to report to the draft board. After taking his physical exam, Malcolm went in for the routine interview with the army psychiatrist. The interview was anything but routine. While most soldiers sat opposite the psychiatrist and answered questions, Malcolm sat shifting around nervously, doing all the talking. He would look suddenly to the right or left, as if to catch someone secretly listening.

Suddenly, he leaped from his chair. He dashed to a door and looked under it, then got to his feet and approached the doctor. He bent and whispered in confidence, and the psychiatrist, unnerved, strained to hear. Could the psychiatrist get him sent directly to the South? He'd have a special mission there: "Organize them nigger soldiers, you dig? Steal us some guns, and kill crackers!"[5] The army decided they could fight the war without Malcolm Little, and he was allowed to return to the streets.

But the streets were becoming much like a war zone for Malcolm. High on cocaine most of his waking hours, suffering from paranoia and constant head colds, he anxiously moved from one cheap Harlem room to the next. He carried a gun and provided anything anyone requested. He fetched and delivered drugs. He sold bootleg liquor and stolen goods. He even robbed and committed burglaries for six months with his stylishly dressed friend Sammy McKnight—also known as Sammy the Pimp—until they had a fight and broke off their partnership. He did have his limits, though, about what he would do to make a buck. "The only thing I could say good for myself . . . was that I did not indulge in hitting anybody over the head."[6]

Then Malcolm was nearly hit over the head himself by a gangster named West Indian Archie. A powerful and violent man respected by the entire Harlem underworld, Archie, working as a gambler, threatened Malcolm. The dispute was over a number Malcolm wrongly "hit" and for which Archie had paid him three hundred dollars. Now Archie wanted the money back. Malcolm, faced with the threat of confrontation, took more drugs. He was saved from certain harm by his old friend Shorty, who spotted Malcolm stumbling along Nicholas Avenue and pulled him into the car and away back to Boston.

Back in Boston, he seemed older than his eighteen years, a man of grim experience, rushing headlong to a violent end. Now he dressed in the most conservative of clothes—he had come a long way since arriving as a country boy from East Lansing just a few years before. His heavy drug use continued; he walked and talked through a seductive fog brought on by constant use of marijuana and cocaine. He formed a burglary ring with

Shorty and another man, and Bea and her younger sister. Bea had since married a white man in Boston but this had not interfered with her time with Malcolm.

On January 12, 1946, the end came to Malcolm's days as Detroit Red. While Malcolm was attempting to reclaim a stolen watch left for repair at a Boston jewelry shop, a plainclothes policeman stepped out of the shadows and arrested him. When the arresting officer turned his back on Malcolm for a moment, Malcolm nearly pulled out his own gun—but something made him hesitate. He simply stiffened. And it was a good thing, too: The man's partner was hiding in the shadows just a few feet away, his own gun out, his finger on the trigger.

As Malcolm was to learn later, the arrest had probably prevented a deadly confrontation at his apartment. Bea's husband had broken into the place while the gang was out and was waiting for them to return so he could confront Malcolm.

In a sense—and Malcolm readily admitted this— going to jail had saved his life. He had made enough people angry enough to want to kill him, and he was getting himself into dangerous new situations every day. But why or how did he escape death on this day twice? "I believe that everything is written," he would later say.[7]

Written, too, was the punishment he would receive. Any first-time felon could expect a fairly reasonable bail. But while the women got a low bail, the men's bail was ten thousand dollars each. Then came the sentencing. The women were sent to prison for one to five years, which meant they could get out after a year had passed. Shorty and Malcolm, though, were not as fortunate. They were convicted on fourteen counts of burglary and possession of stolen goods. A first offense on burglary usually brought a two-year sentence; Malcolm and Shorty received eight to ten years. "The judge told me to my face," Malcolm later recalled, " 'This will teach you to stay away from white girls.' "[8]

Prison

When Malcolm Little arrived at damp, dark Charlestown State Prison near Boston in early 1946, he was not quite twenty-one years old. He would later declare that this was the very lowest time in his life.

Malcolm spent his first year in Charlestown as a troublesome inmate. Deprived of marijuana and cocaine, he was often irritable. He drank nutmeg, a spice from the prison kitchen that gave a marijuanalike high when it was mixed with water. He was insolent to certain guards. He lashed out at the prison psychologists. And his open hostility towards organized religion won him the nickname "Satan" from other Charlestown inmates.

One prisoner, however, was more curious than offended at Malcolm's wild talk and behavior. John Elton Bembry, or Bimbi as he was known, was an older black man in Charlestown for burglary. Intelligent and soft-spoken, Bimbi was respected by all inmates for his kindness and ability to win arguments. To Malcolm, Bimbi was a revelation, "the first man I had ever seen command total respect . . . with his words."[1]

Malcolm introduced himself to Bimbi. According to an account by author Bruce Perry, as Bimbi and another man sat playing dominoes in the prison yard, Malcolm walked over and bumped Bimbi. The dominoes scattered and fell in the dirt.

Malcolm, offering no apology, circled and came back. Now Bimbi stood up, ready to defend himself. There was a moment's hesitation. Suddenly the other domino player greeted Malcolm, calling him "Satan." Malcolm nodded to the man, then blurted out to Bimbi that he was sorry. Then Malcolm suddenly launched into a series of heated questions about religion: Did Bimbi believe in the Christian God? In God the Father, Son, and Holy Ghost? ". . . and all that crap?"[2] That day Bimbi answered as best he could, and as time passed the two men gradually became friends.

Bimbi did not always say things that Malcolm found agreeable. Some time later, when Bimbi told Malcolm that he had brains and ought to use them, Malcolm balked. Malcolm would say, years later, that he was not very receptive to this kind of advice. It sounded like a criticism from one of his old teachers back in Lansing.

But Malcolm accepted Bimbi's advice and started to

educate himself. He began spending time in the prison library. He continued to follow Bimbi around, now asking him about the things he was discovering in books. He took a correspondence course in English grammar, then one in Latin, to understand the roots of the English language.

What absorbed Malcolm most was his discovery of black history. He was astonished with what he began to learn about the historical treatment of blacks by whites. He was outraged by the overwhelming evidence of black suffering, and as his reading expanded, so did his awareness of white cruelty toward blacks.

He also marveled at books that discussed the advances and wonders of African civilizations, including the flowering of ancient Egypt. Most popular history books, he found, emphasized only the history of whites. "I found out that the history-whitening process . . . had left out great things that black men had done. . . ."[3]

He grew feverish with study; he could not get enough of books. When darkness came and the prison's indoor lights were shut, Malcolm would bring out a book and huddle against the door of his cell, straining to read by the pale light from way down the hall, where the guards stayed. Reading in this light strained his eyes severely enough that he soon needed prescription glasses.

He also worked on improving his writing skills and expanding his vocabulary. He took no shortcuts, either. As filmmaker Spike Lee recently commented, "you see him going through the dictionary, copying every single word and definition, A to Z."[4]

Being absorbed in self-education, though, did not keep him from everyday prison life. Malcolm acted as a bookie at Charlestown, arranging other inmates' bets on horse races and boxing matches, while keeping a percentage of each bet for himself. He spent his income on nutmeg obtained from his contacts in the kitchen. Like many black prisoners, he cheered for Jackie Robinson in 1947 when the black Brooklyn Dodger became the first to integrate the white man's game. And like any prisoner, he was subject to being transferred, which happened in January 1947, when he was sent to nearby Concord Reformatory.

One day while at Concord, Malcolm received a mysterious letter from his brother Reginald. Reginald, two years younger than Malcolm, announced to his older brother that he had become involved with a religious group in Chicago.

Malcolm had gotten letters like this before from other members of his family—Wilfred, Hilda, and Philbert were already part of the Chicago group. Malcolm had angrily dismissed their letters, telling them to keep their religion to themselves. But he felt close to Reginald and read his letter with curiosity—especially the passage that advised him that if he, Malcolm, were to swear off pork and stop smoking cigarettes, he could get out of prison. Malcolm snapped at the bait; he made up his mind quickly.

At the next meal when pork was served, Malcolm refused his portion. Other prisoners stopped eating to look. Soon the whole prison was talking about "Satan's" strange behavior. Author Bruce Perry reports Malcolm later recalling that he felt "very proud."[5] Though Malcolm was not sure why. The answer was to come a short while later, after he had been transferred, by his own request, to Norfolk Prison.

Norfolk, a clean and modern facility, was for prisoners who had behaved well in other facilities. To Malcolm, Norfolk was a paradise. There were showers on every floor. Inmates could tend outdoor garden plots. Outside, too, there were playing fields. Most precious to Malcolm, though, was the lavish prison library, donated by a state senator.

Malcolm emerged from his scholarly world when Reginald at last arrived to visit. Reginald wasted no time in revealing why he had instructed Malcolm to give up pork and tobacco. He told Malcolm that according to the religion of Islam, Muslims were forbidden by God, or Allah, to eat pork. Tobacco, too, was to be avoided. Then Reginald began to tell Malcolm about the group that he, Reginald, and their siblings already belonged to, called the Nation of Islam.

The Nation of Islam was created in the wake of the appearance in Detroit, in the 1930s, of a mysterious man named Wallace Fard.[6] Fard was small—about five foot five—with tan skin and vaguely Oriental features. He sold silks door-to-door in Detroit's black ghetto which was called, inappropriately enough, Paradise Valley.

Many poor residents of Paradise Valley were attracted to Fard; they accepted him as a teacher or minister. But Fard told his closest followers that he was Mahdi, or God, on a divine mission to teach American blacks about their African and Islamic heritage. He claimed that blacks were the first people to rule the world and would soon return to proudly rule it again.

While Fard drew upon many ideas from traditional Islam, his own teachings were decidedly different. For one thing, traditional Islam has Muhammad, who had lived in the seventh century, as its prophet; Fard was to designate one of his followers as His Last Messenger. For another, traditional Islam teaches love and brotherhood among all the races; according to Fard, whites could not be loved—they were devils.

Fard's teachings were unique in other ways. Once the world was made up only of blacks, claimed Fard, but then whites had been created by a black, big-headed mad scientist named Yacub. Through genetic experimentation, Yacub was able to breed all pigmentation from the race of black "Originals." From the superior black race came the inferior brown man, the red man, the yellow man, and finally the white man, who was the evilest of all.

Fard explained that these evil whites had lived in caves and walked on all fours while the blacks were building empires and writing poetry. Then, six thousand years ago, the whites came out of their caves and became civilized, and soon took over the world. These white devils were allowed by God, or Allah, to rule for six thousand years.

At the end of the six thousand years (which was to have arrived early in this century), the white race would be destroyed. A man-made planet, called "The Mother Ship," would descend from space and call all blacks to come aboard. Those blacks who refused were doomed to die with the whites. Then, natural disasters would strike the continent. Great tidal waves would push the population into the middle of the country to be destroyed by poisonous bombs dropped from small planes piloted by children who had never smiled. For centuries, the atmosphere would burn; it would take an even longer time for the earth to cool off. For a thousand years there would be no life on earth; then, the children of the Original People would return by spaceship to rule the planet again.

One of the men with whom Fard shared his secrets was a small, frail Detroit autoworker named Elijah Poole. Poole, like Malcolm's father, had come from Georgia and had a minimum of education. He was awed by Fard, and recognized some great power the other man had. "I recognized him to be God in person and that is

In 1934, Elijah Muhammad (pictured here, speaking) took over the Nation of Islam. Over the years, membership declined and rose, and the Nation was in and out of the public eye, but the message remained the same: the white man is the devil.

what he said he was, but he forbade me to tell anyone else."[7] Elijah Poole became Elijah Muhammad, and he and Fard worked to further the cause of the Nation of Islam.

They began attracting urban followers—usually poor blacks who had emigrated from the South and were disappointed by big-city life—and establishing mosques in converted storefronts in cities throughout the Midwest. By 1934, there were over 8,000 members of the organization Fard called the "Lost-Found Nation of Islam," or simply the "Nation of Islam."

When Fard mysteriously disappeared in 1934, Elijah Muhammad took over the Nation of Islam. Over the years, membership declined and rose, and the Nation was in and out of the public eye, but the message remained the same: the white man is the Devil.

As Reginald explained the Nation of Islam to Malcolm, Malcolm was ready to hear it. He sat, listening intently. And after only five minutes or so of Reginald's explanation of the doctrine according to Elijah Muhammad, Malcolm was transformed.

It was, in the words of author Peter Goldman, "a blinding, shattering conversion."[8] The twisted path of his own life before prison suddenly made sense to Malcolm. There was a cause for all Malcolm's suffering: the white man. The white man was the enemy. The white man had enslaved blacks and made them forget their accomplishments, their pride, their superiority; the white man was the devil. Malcolm's own lengthy prison term was proof of the white man's cruelty towards blacks. ". . . when my brother told me that God had taught Mr. Elijah Muhammad that the white race was a race of Devils, my eyes came open on the spot," Malcolm would later recall.[9] He decided to devote his life to Elijah Muhammad and the Nation of Islam.

That Malcolm, or anyone, could believe stories of mother ships descending from the heavens and unsmiling children at the controls of spaceships is troubling to many. But writer Peter Goldman, commenting upon the beliefs of the Nation of Islam, points out that to fundamentalist believers—believers who accept a doctrine word for word—a spaceship bringing the gospel is not a far cry from "the parting of the Red Sea or the miracle of the loaves and fishes."[10]

Followers found a sense of respect in the Nation's codes of conduct.[11] All members of the Nation were taught to abstain from pork, tobacco, and alcohol, and to practice thriftiness and cleanliness.

For some, like Malcolm, codes of conduct and religion were not necessarily the most important aspects of the Nation's teachings. Author Robert Vernon says that the teachings "could well have been of Black Buddhism or Black Brahmanism or Black Anything with equal effect."[12] What was important was the declared contempt of and war on the white man. While the Nation of Islam taught blacks to love and respect themselves, it also insisted that the white man was the enemy. Author Peter Goldman agrees that this was an idea that could help poor urban American blacks understand "why one lives in a rat-ridden slum and works, if at all, carrying the white man's baggage and diapering the white man's babies."[13]

To prepare for his life after prison, Malcolm corresponded with his family, then Elijah Muhammad himself, in order to learn more fully about his beliefs. Elijah Muhammad responded warmly. He sent Malcolm elaborate letters and even a little spending money, as he did with all convicts who wrote to him. Malcolm was terribly grateful. To him, Elijah Muhammad and his teachings had saved him, had "reached down into the mud to lift me up, to save me from being what I inevitably would have been: a dead criminal in a grave, or, if still alive, a flint-hard, bitter, thirty-seven-year-old convict in some penitentiary, or insane asylum. Or, at best, I would have been an old fading Detroit Red, hustling, stealing enough for food and narcotics, and myself being stalked as prey by cruelly ambitious younger hustlers such as Detroit Red had been."[14]

Malcolm was a changed man. He continued his formidable reading program, digging hungrily now through volumes of history and philosophy for evidence of the white race's evil. He learned to pray. He took part in organized debates and improved his ability to win arguments and convert other convicts to his point of view. He quit all his vices and became a model prisoner. He spent his remaining five or so years in prison preparing for his release, which came on August 7, 1952.

He had entered prison as Malcolm Little, hustler, addict, and convicted burglar. He left prison as Malcolm X—in his own words, "Ex-smoker. Ex-drinker. Ex-Christian. Ex-slave."[15]

5

Building With Words

In 1952, when Malcolm X re-entered the world after being a prisoner for eight years, the civil rights movement had hardly been born. Martin Luther King, Jr. was a doctoral student at Boston University. The landmark case of *Brown* v. *Board of Education of Topeka*, which would end in a decision against school segregation, was just beginning its way up to the Supreme Court. Protests against civil rights injustices occurred, for the most part, in the courts, not in the streets, and they were carried out in a peaceful fashion and with the goal of all people living equally and together under the same law.

The Nation of Islam puttered along in American cities, barely a visible presence. As author Peter Goldman describes it, at the beginning of the 1950s the Nation was "a communion of possibly four hundred souls scattered among storefront mosques and front-parlor missions in Detroit, Chicago, Washington, Harlem, and possibly a half-dozen other places."[1] Though only four hundred souls strong, the Nation of Islam boasted a general discipline, determination, and order strong enough to frighten black Christians. And the Nation's membership would soon begin to rise dramatically.

Fresh out of prison, staying with his brother Wilbert's family in Detroit and working in a local furniture store, Malcolm studied Islam and attended meetings at Temple Number One, located in a downtown storefront. Malcolm was eager to see and meet Elijah Muhammad himself, and at one of the large rallies, held at the Nation's Temple Number Two in Chicago, he got his chance.

Elijah Muhammad had just finished his sermon. He had told the audience how understanding his teachings would allow them to understand who they were, and how to avoid the coming destruction of the world, whose "complete disintegration is both imminent and inescapable. Any man who integrates with the world must share in its disintegration and destruction. If the Black man would listen, he need not be a part of this certain doom."[2]

Now, the frail Elijah Muhammad looked over the crowd and called Malcolm's name. Malcolm stood up, stunned. Elijah Muhammad then spoke with pride of

Malcolm as he looked after his release from prison. Appearing intense and determined, he probably posed for this photograph shortly after he joined the Nation of Islam.

Malcolm's struggle to learn and spread the doctrine in prison. "I believe that he is going to remain faithful," Muhammad told the audience.[3]

Afterwards, Malcolm and his family drove to the Muslim leader's mansion, to which they had been invited for dinner. Malcolm met men with names like James 2X or Robert 20X—the number in front of the X identifying them as the second or twentieth man with the same first name who had been accepted into the Nation. He witnessed the politeness and respect the temple members showed towards one another and towards their host, Elijah Muhammad.

Malcolm waited for a private moment, then went over to speak with Elijah Muhammad. What was the best way to attract new members to the organization? he asked Muhammad. To this question Elijah Muhammad responded: "Go after the young people. Once you get them, the older ones will follow through shame."[4] This statement struck a chord in Malcolm. Not long after that momentous meeting, Malcolm quit his job in the furniture store and became an assistant minister in the Nation of Islam. He began seeking out potential converts on the Detroit streets and in the bars, among ex-convicts and those out of work. He talked to them and to their friends and to anybody who would listen. Malcolm's dedication and unbending loyalty to the Nation, as well as his talents as a speaker, became increasingly apparent to Elijah Muhammad.

Malcolm found it easy to communicate with blacks from various walks of life. He had lived on the street and knew its language, as well as the language of the underworld and of the prison—the slang, the catchwords, the hipster phrases. He had also learned a good bit of history and philosophy and could appeal to university students and better-educated blacks as well. He was consistently "direct and to the point and could be understood on all educational levels."[5]

From listening to other skilled speakers—including Elijah Muhammad—Malcolm became practiced in effective ways to make a point. One thing he had learned was how to take an accepted phrase and humorously stand it on its head. When he told fellow Muslims "We didn't land on Plymouth Rock. Plymouth Rock landed on *us!*"[6] the listeners would recognize and appreciate the humor and irony and truth under the clever turn of phrase.

Another effective technique Malcolm learned was the use of analogy—a way of making essentially different things similar. One day, Elijah Muhammad, wanting to teach Malcolm that the best way to change people was not to criticize them but to show them a better way, placed a dirty drinking glass on a table next to a clean glass. The best way to spread his teachings, Muhammad said, was not to condemn a person if you see him or her with a dirty glass: ". . . just show them the clean glass of water that you have. When they inspect it, you won't have to say that yours is better."[7]

Malcolm learned fast. And as a result of his tremendous energy and perseverance, the membership of Detroit's Temple Number One tripled within a few months, and Malcolm was quickly promoted to higher responsibilities within the organization. Soon, he was regularly recruiting enough members to open temples in Boston, Philadelphia, and other cities. In June, 1954, only two years after his release from prison, Malcolm moved to New York and took over as minister of Mosque Number Seven, located in a four-story building in Harlem.

Malcolm quickly became a pest to other religious leaders in Harlem. He would stand outside a church with some of his followers and wait respectfully for the service to end. As the parishioners filed out of the church, he and his followers would introduce themselves by telling the parishioners they were fools to believe in the "white man's religion." Some people chuckled, others grew angry, but many were curious. They would follow Malcolm and his men back to the temple, to hear what they had to say. The preacher would complain, but there was very little he could do.

Having "captured" his audience, Malcolm knew how to tailor his speeches to them. Anticipating some suspicion among the Christian listeners, he would think of something to say from the Bible. "Better to be laughed at and be safe from the storm [like Noah] than to be caught in the storm just because you didn't want to be laughed at."[8] Hearing his familiarity with the Bible, his audience would feel more at ease and trusting.

He then might ask the black Christians to take a good look at the white man who gave them their religion. "This blue-eyed devil has twisted his Christianity, to keep his foot on our backs . . . to keep our eyes fixed on the pie in the sky and heaven in the hereafter . . . while *he* enjoys *his* heaven right *here* . . . on *this earth* . . . in *this life*."[9]

There was no doubt in Malcolm's mind that Islam was superior to Christianity, and he impressed this upon everybody he tried to convert. One humorous anecdote, related by writer Louis Lomax, cites the seriousness and morality of Malcolm in the Nation of Islam:

> Malcolm was said to have been trying to convert a black Baptist to Islam, and he was asked by the man what he needed to do.
> "Well," Malcolm said, "my brother, you have to stop drinking, stop swearing, stop gambling, stop using dope, and stop cheating on your wife!"
> "Hell," the convert replied, "I think I had better remain a Christian."[10]

When delivering a sermon to temple members only, Malcolm did not have to be careful to avoid offending any listeners; to the converted, he would use his strongest language. He would call his enemies "white

Devils" and their government "wicked."[11] One phonograph record made at the time reveals him as saying white people resembled animals, characterizing them as "reptiles" and laughing at their "stringy, dog-like hair."[12]

The members of the temple would at first listen respectfully, men on one side of the room, wearing crisp white shirts and bow ties, and women on the other side, dressed in traditional Muslim dresses and with their heads covered. Soon, as his speech would move them, they would urge him on, shouting back at him to "Teach, Messenger!" and "Tell 'em!"

He might hold up a photo of a black hanging victim. "Who hung this man on this tree?" he'd ask. "Your white Christian brother. Who raped your mother and stood her up in the market while they felt her body to see if she was a good breeder and then sold her away from her family? The white man brags about these things in the library. He has made you so blind that you sit and read this and say, 'Oh, that's about people years ago.' They are still hanging black men on trees."[13]

And who was the white devil's greatest enemy? Elijah Muhammad. The devil white man, Malcolm declared, *"does not want the Honorable Elijah Muhammad stirring awake the sleeping giant of you and me, and all of our ignorant, brainwashed kind here in the white man's heaven and the black man's hell here in the wilderness of North America!"*[14]

He would close the meeting the same way each time, thanking Allah, the one God, and Elijah Muhammad, his servant and apostle. Then he would raise his hand for all to be dismissed. He would tell them to seek peace "but if anyone attacks you, we do not teach you to turn the other cheek. May Allah bless you to be successful and victorious in all that you do."[15]

In time, his popularity in Harlem grew. Other leaders from mainstream civil rights organizations like the Congress of Racial Equality (CORE) and the National Association for the Advancement of Colored People (NAACP) would hold rallies before respectable crowds, but when Malcolm spoke, the streets were packed with two or three times as many listeners. These were blacks from all walks of life in Harlem, and they were curious to hear the tall young man speak.

They would hear him emphasize the need for blacks to get rid of destructive behavior. "Stop carrying guns and knives to harm each other," he'd say. "Stop drinking whiskey, taking dope, reefers, and even cigarettes. No more gambling! Save your money. Stop fornication, adultery and prostitution. Elevate the black woman; respect her and protect her. Let us rid ourselves of immoral habits and God will be with us to protect and guide us."[16]

They would see him share the podium with whites, in the cause of black morality. At one Harlem rally, many white elected officials were seated along with Malcolm before a banner that condemned "narcotic gangsters," hoodlums, and prostitutes as "destroying the fabrics of society." Other speakers spoke out against these evils. When Malcolm got up to speak, he made it a point to condemn the police department—composed mainly of whites—as well: "Dope, prostitution, and numbers could not flourish here in Harlem without the knowledge of the police!"[17]

They would listen to him preach the Nation's message of segregation. He would insist that the white man was doomed, and that those who followed the white man were only fooling themselves. ". . . those Uncle Tom, brainwashed, white-minded Negroes who love you may do it [integrate], but the masses of black people want a society of their own in a land of their own."[18]

And this urge for segregation struck a chord with many blacks whose hopes for equality had risen and fallen over the years. They had felt elation at the 1954 *Brown* v. *Board of Education of Topeka* ruling that ended official segregation for the nation's schoolchildren, but the ruling had not been enforced. Black children were still being denied entry to white schools. And while their history books had told them they had been freed by the Civil War, one hundred years later, as they looked around, they perceived that they were free only to live in ghettos and in rural poverty.

To all his black audiences, Malcolm offered a voice. He said things they couldn't say, or didn't want to say, or were afraid to say, and they appreciated him for this.

Malcolm X addressing a Harlem rally against crime. Several times in his career he shared the platform with civic leaders and elected officials sympathetic to his views on the problems confronting the black community and how to solve them.

He was able to get them to free the anger they kept bottled up, and he freed them up to feel and think about themselves, where they were and where they had come from. And often they were overcome with a sense of dignity and pride, and thankfulness, watching him speak and gesture and smile down on them from the podium.

Individuals felt changed after meeting personally with him, too, whether in the streets or the bars of Harlem, or in the restaurants, grocery stores, and cafés that the Nation of Islam had begun to establish there. Photographer Robert Haggins recalls[19] one such meeting he had with Malcolm in the 1950s:

Haggins worked for a New York newspaper. After a dispute between the New York City police department and the Harlem Temple, he was sent to get an interview with Malcolm X, whom he'd never heard of.

Haggins went to the 22nd Street Café in Harlem to meet Malcolm, on the pretense of wanting background material about the Nation. After Malcolm gave Haggins the required information, Malcolm asked him about his name. "Where does the name 'Haggins' come from?"

"It's part Irish, I guess," answered Haggins. "And part English."

"You mean you were owned by an Irish man and an English man, right?" asked Malcolm. "Now, don't get angry with me," he continued, "think about what I'm saying to you. Words come from someplace. Like the word Negro. Negro is Necro, meaning something without life, something dead. . . . I'm saying stop that! Don't be a dead man—be a live man. You got your name from a slave! Drop your name—you're an African!"

The meeting with Malcolm stunned Haggins. "On my way home," the photographer recalls, "it just kept turning over and over in my mind, the things he said."

Soon after this meeting, Haggins quit his job on the newspaper and went to work as Malcolm's personal photographer, devoting all his time to being ready to photograph the Muslim leader when asked to. "He was my mentor, my teacher, everything," says Haggins, smiling at the memory. "He taught me to be disciplined. One thing Negroes need is to be disciplined."

Malcolm's words also made many enemies. Whites who heard or heard of him heard the defiant voice of an angry minority claiming not to need the white man. Malcolm's voice scared them.

Malcolm also made an enemy of the United States government. In 1953, the FBI began watching Malcolm and his activities. They put listening devices in the places he frequented and planted spies in his audiences. Malcolm's voice concerned them.

Black leaders in the civil rights movement became enemies, too. Men like Whitney Young, Bayard Rustin, and Martin Luther King, Jr. frowned when they heard Malcolm accusing them of loving the white man and of meekly waiting until the white man got around to treating them better. Malcolm's voice annoyed them.

Some black leaders spoke out against the Nation of Islam. Thurgood Marshall, who was chief legal counsel for the NAACP and who would later sit on the Supreme Court, remarked that the Nation was "run by a bunch of thugs organized from prisons and jails and financed, I am sure, by [Egyptian president Gamal Abdel] Nasser or some Arab group."[20] Roy Wilkins of the same organization railed not only against white extremists but all ". . . Negro extremists preaching against white people simply for the sake of whiteness."[21]

For the enemies of the Nation of Islam, Malcolm had nothing but scorn. Allah would punish them. All blacks, claimed Malcolm, should distance themselves from whites. Blacks should just stand back and watch as the white man destroyed himself and was destroyed by Allah.

And his enemies in the civil rights movement scorned him in return. They condemned Malcolm and the Nation for standing on the sidelines, for criticizing and only talking a good fight, for not raising a finger. For not getting involved.

And Malcolm ignored this criticism. He called his critics fools and their efforts useless. With the Johnson Hinton episode of 1957, he also showed Harlem that the Muslims were indeed more than just talkers.

But talking had brought him to prominence. His words had built up the Nation. As John Henrik Clarke asserts, "He was principally a speaker and his style was one of the most effective of any orator in this century."[22]

In the Spotlight

With Malcolm's help, the Nation of Islam organization
had flourished in the 1950s. By the end of that decade
there were fifty Nation of Islam temples in operation
throughout the country; at one point during the decade,
the value of the combined assets of the Nation of Islam
was put at ten million dollars.[1] Elijah Muhammad
himself lived in an eighteen-room Victorian mansion on
Chicago's South Side.

Malcolm's home in New York was much smaller. He
and Betty X (born Betty Sanders), a member of the
Harlem mosque, were married in January 1958 and
moved to a quiet street in the East Elmhurst section of
Queens, New York, into a modest house owned by the
Nation; their house had a living room, two bedrooms,

and a kitchen. The couple had their first child, a daughter named Attilah, near the end of the year.

His devotion to Betty was strong. Busy at work for the temple, Malcolm would call her many times during the day, just to check in with her. And he would always tell others how he trusted Betty: "She's the only person I'd trust with my life. That means I trust her more than I do myself."[2]

He was also devoted to his mentor. Throughout the 1950s, nobody who saw them together or heard Malcolm's overflowing praise of his mentor could doubt that Malcolm would give his own life for Elijah Muhammad. Some scholars even suggest that Elijah Muhammad represented the father Malcolm had lost early in life.

Included in Malcolm's duties now was acting as ambassador for the Nation of Islam, in which capacity he was required to travel outside America. Malcolm first visited Africa in July of 1959. He was sent to get the feel of the land, in advance of Elijah Muhammad's visit to that part of the world. Upon his return to New York, Malcolm said he was "well-accepted by Muslims and that the Muslims in Egypt and Africa are blacker than me."[3]

What he did not mention upon his return, however, was that he had seen Muslims of many different colors—not only darker but lighter than himself. He mentioned nothing of light-skinned Muslims, or even the blond, blue-eyed Muslims, both of whom were not at all unusual outside America. Though faced with the disturbing fact of white Muslims—for if the white man was the devil, how could he also be a Muslim?—Malcolm did not acknowledge or discuss it.

While Malcolm had been out of the country in 1959, though, the American people also witnessed something disturbing. From July 13 to the 17th, a television program narrated by Mike Wallace called "The Hate That Hate Produced" was shown in five installments, one each night for five nights. Malcolm had encouraged the project and was featured in the series, while Elijah Muhammad, less enthusiastic for the publicity, had to be talked into it.

Until this broadcast, the majority of white Americans knew only one kind of organized black protest against racism: that of direct action. Direct action often took the form of peaceful marches or boycotts and occurred most noticeably in the South. Direct action groups like the Congress of Racial Equality, the NAACP, and the Southern Christian Leadership Conference would peacefully break civic laws, and the arrests of their members and the violence often committed against them by local police made headlines and won public sympathy. While many whites saw leaders like Martin Luther King, Jr., Bayard Rustin, and Roy Wilkins as radical forces to be feared, many more could feel for King and his associates, who marched peacefully, who included whites in their protest, who talked about nonviolent change and the urgent need for black civil rights.

On their television sets in this summer in 1959 white Americans saw a different set of blacks, blacks whose protests against racism were nondirect. These blacks did not formally attack racism through the courts or through electoral politics. These blacks looked down upon whites, reviling them for their crimes against the world, and they declared they didn't need whites. These blacks declared defiantly that no action was necessary: the fall of the white man—"the white devil"—was imminent. For five nights in a row, television audiences across the country witnessed the workings of a militant organization right in their midst. They learned of an elementary school in Chicago called the University of Islam, where well-behaved, well-dressed children were taught that whites were devils. They beheld the frail but authoritative prophet, Elijah Muhammad. And they shivered at the words of his minister, Malcolm X.

Now the Nation of Islam was in the national spotlight. Magazines like *Time, Newsweek,* and *Life* ran features on the organization. A young black scholar named C. Eric Lincoln wrote a book called *The Black Muslims,* which also garnered attention for the organization; the American press began referring to the Nation of Islam as the Black Muslims. While Malcolm never gave away specific details about how the broadcast affected the rise in membership in the Nation of Islam, it can be assumed that it was high—one source says 10,000 was probably the membership at its peak of popularity.[4] And there were many more who didn't join the ranks but were sympathetic to the message.

While Malcolm thought that the documentary was too one-sided, showing the Nation in a hateful posture, he was glad for the publicity. He wanted to reach as many people as possible with it. And the publicity almost always centered on him. Everywhere one looked, it seemed, there was an image of Malcolm X glaring out from the cover of a newspaper or magazine. There was the pointing finger, the chin jutting out in defiance, the eyes focused and hard, the brilliant teeth clenched in anger and rage.

Those who spent much time around Malcolm were disturbed by his media image. As Robert Haggins, Malcolm's personal photographer, recalls, "The media didn't want to see another side of Malcolm. They only wanted the sneering, finger-pointing shot of him.

"Malcolm played a game with me one time. He said 'watch my speech today. About ten minutes into the speech, I'm going to find something to be angry about. See if the photographers don't start using their cameras then.'

"For the first ten minutes of the speech, the other photographers sat on their hands. No one snapped a picture. Then X began getting angry about something, and I could see them all reach for their cameras and begin snapping away."

Even Malcolm's children became part of the image. A widely circulated photo of Malcolm and his daughter Attilah shows the young girl scowling at the camera, as if she inherited her father's rage. But photographer Haggins reveals the story behind the image: "Attilah was scowling at me—because I was the one taking the picture. I was the one distracting her daddy from paying attention to her. That's the reason she's making that face."[5]

But Malcolm did much to promote his image as a hatemonger. He regularly visited the reporters who had first sought him out; now he came to them with shocking statements that he knew they couldn't resist printing. For example, he told reporters, "I rejoice when a white man dies!"[6] Of course this statement was included in an article. Yet, in private, he was almost always cordial to the white newspapermen who copied down his words.

His image as a hatemonger extended to other minority groups. Though he expressed admiration for Jews and praised their achievement in reclaiming the land of Israel after the horrors of the Holocaust, he publicly chastised them for controlling too much business in Harlem. He called them "yids." He asserted that as white devils, they were the worst.

In private, though, he was sensitive to being called

anti-Semitic. According to author Bruce Perry, he remarked to one accuser that he wasn't against all Jews, but that he was just using them as a convenient symbol.[7]

His main purpose now was to spread the message of Elijah Muhammad. And if being an angry black man accomplished this, then he would oblige. As writer and journalist Peter Goldman insists, "Malcolm created himself. But we did find him irresistible, and, through us and our media, he reached that other country called Black America."[8]

He was able to reach both white and black America by accepting speaking engagements around the country. University debates were especially challenging. At first, he would be terribly nervous until it was time to go on stage—he would sweat and pace, and sometimes he told others he didn't want to go through with it at all. But in time he learned to calm down. Determined to be as well-prepared as possible, he would practice in his hotel room by taking both sides of an issue, arguing one against the other. Author Bruce Perry claims that Malcolm would also turn on the television and study the tactics of lawyers in courtroom dramas.[9]

On stage he put his tactics into action. One tactic was the defensive strategy of turning the questions of opponents around to put them on the defensive. If an opponent accusingly asked "Does the Nation of Islam support the government of the United States?" Malcolm would respond "Does the government of the United

States support the Nation of Islam?" The opponent would usually be caught off guard for a few moments, and the audience would often cheer Malcolm's refusal to be cornered.

He always worked on his ability to craft his speeches to his various listeners. He claimed to have learned how to feel out his audience with what he called his "psychic radar."[10] Debating at a university with a largely white student body, he would be charming and humorous and try to refrain from talking about the destruction by whites. At Boston University, after an argumentative question and answer period, he apologized to his audience for having raised his voice.[11]

While tempering his voice before university audiences, back in New York Malcolm lashed out at his enemies—especially the civil rights movement's leaders, whom he claimed were controlled by whites. A local radio audience heard him accuse black leaders of "praying for those who spitefully use them, and anytime a person believes in a teaching like that and practices it, it doesn't make them an intelligent person or a man, it makes him a fool and a coward. . . ."[12] And any black leader who said anything negative in return about the Nation would meet with Malcolm's wrath. After Roy Wilkins, Executive Director of the NAACP, had criticized the Nation, Malcolm angrily denounced Wilkins for "parroting what he has been told to say or paid to say by those who have control over him."[13]

The idea of fighting for civil rights annoyed Malcolm, for according to Elijah Muhammad's teachings, all the black man needed to do was to keep apart from the white man and watch him be destroyed by Allah.

At the same time, though, he was not entirely comfortable with this stance. It was difficult to sit back and watch. He had always been active in making changes, whether it was moving to Boston and Harlem as a teenager, educating himself in prison, or building the Nation itself.

There were a few times when Malcolm dropped his attacks against other leaders. At a Harlem street rally in the spring of 1960, he addressed the need for unity among the country's black leaders, saying that despite their differences "the hour is too short today for black people to afford the luxury of 'differences' "[14]

Wanting to be active about generating change spurred him on to find a way of his own to practice what he preached about black economic self-sufficiency. He first agreed to write a weekly column for Harlem's *Amsterdam News*; pleased with the success of these columns, he founded a newspaper called *Muhammad Speaks!* This paper, created in the basement of Malcolm's East Elmhurst home, became the organ of the Nation of Islam and featured Malcolm's own writing. The newspaper was sold by blacks in black urban communities, first in New York, then across the country.

Profits from the newspaper went into Muslim-owned businesses, like restaurants and grocery stores in black communities.

While Elijah Muhammad was pleased with Malcolm's hard work for the Nation, he gradually became less at ease with his disciple's notoriety. Besides being eclipsed from public view, Elijah Muhammad was uncomfortable with Malcolm's more abrasive statements, especially when they attacked the government. Muhammad did not want the Nation of Islam to have a negative public image nor to make an enemy of the U.S. government. Elijah Muhammad did not want the actions of his organization or his comfortable life-style intruded upon in any way.

There were others in the Nation of Islam who had problems with Malcolm's popularity. Elijah Muhammad's children, who had powerful positions in the Nation, resented Malcolm's popularity and even feared a family takeover: Malcolm's brother Wilfred headed Detroit's Temple Number One, and Philbert had been placed in control of Michigan temples in Lansing, Grand Rapids, Flint, and Saginaw. Others in the organization were upset, too, when they were passed over for the title of national minister, which Malcolm received in 1962. According to author Bruce Perry, jealous members began trying to create conflicts between the Prophet and Malcolm X.[15]

Hard at work building the Nation, Malcolm ignored

any conflicts he heard about and tried to find time for his family. A second daughter, Qubilah, was born to Malcolm and Betty on December 25, 1960. There was a sense of stability in his life now. He would kiss his wife and children in the morning, climb into his blue Oldsmobile, and head into the city, along with hundreds of thousands of other New York commuters.

When with family or friends, out of the public eye, Malcolm relaxed and let others see the usually hidden parts of his personality. One of the men who was with him often at this time was Benjamin Karim, a member of the Harlem Mosque. According to Karim, Malcolm used to love banana splits and could down several, one after the other. "He would tell jokes . . . he would discuss things just like you and I would, so that you saw the human side of the man as opposed to the idol that the public made of him."[16]

He also tried to hide some sides of his personality from the media and grew angry with himself the few times he let himself slip. During an interview in which he was talking about his experiences in the Harlem nightlife, he suddenly rose from his chair and grabbed a nearby radiator for a partner and began lindy-hopping in one place, arms and legs pumping wildly, happily self-absorbed for a few moments. Catching himself in this show of undisciplined behavior, he just as suddenly returned to his chair and sat sullenly until the interview was over.

Malcolm with his daughters Attilah and Qubilah. Malcolm took obvious pleasure in the time he spent with his children.

But "slipups" like this were merely leaves in the forest of his tremendous accomplishment. Once dismissed by a schoolteacher for wishing to become a lawyer, he had gone through hell and risen up to become, in the early years of the 1960s, "an advocate for an entire people."[17]

The Need for Action

On Friday night, April 27th, 1962, in Los Angeles, California, after a meeting at the Muslim mosque, two black workers from a drycleaning establishment one block away were unloading suits from a car to take into their store. A police car manned by two white policemen drove up to question them, probably suspecting burglary or theft. A scuffle broke out, members of the mosque came to see what was happening, a shot was fired, and an alarm went off. When additional police cars arrived they converged not on the scene of the scuffle but on the mosque itself.

The white policemen, surrounded by Muslims, pulled out their guns. Gunfire erupted. Seven Muslims and one policeman were wounded. One Muslim, a Korean War veteran named Ronald Stokes, was apparently walking towards the police unarmed, hands stretched out before him, when he was shot. Stokes died.

The next day, an enraged Malcolm got the word that he was to fly out to Los Angeles. He knew a confrontation with the police was inevitable, for the Muslims had been preaching self-defense for years, and police were always hassling them. But before Malcolm departed, Elijah Muhammad gave his disciple careful instructions: Don't start anything. Do not fall into their trap.

Malcolm was frustrated. He wanted revenge. But he saw the wisdom in his mentor's orders and followed them. In Los Angeles he spoke out angrily against the violence, but did not call for retribution. At the end of the week, he conducted the traditional Muslim funeral for Stokes, a quiet and solemn affair with mints handed out to make the memory of the departed a sweet one. Back in New York, Malcolm had restrained words of warning for the killers of Ronald Stokes: ". . . we do believe that God, our God, the Supreme Being, whose proper name is Allah, will execute judgment and justice in whatever way He sees fit, against the people who are guilty of this crime against our people in this country."[1]

As it turned out, charges against the policeman who shot Stokes were dropped. In court testimony, the officer said he was trying to stop Stokes from advancing. The coroner backed up the officer, labeling Stokes's death as justifiable. The other officers were cleared of charges, too. Eight Muslims, though, were charged with assault.

The Stokes incident frustrated Malcolm. The Muslims had, in a sense, lost face. Their claims that Muslims protected one another and that no one touched the hair on the head of a Muslim were a bit weaker, now. Nonetheless the birth of Malcolm and Betty's third daughter, Ilyasah, brought pleasure and joy at this time of frustration.

In June 1962, Malcolm got some revenge for the Stokes incident. An airplane carrying 120 white Atlantans crashed just after takeoff from Paris; nearly all the passengers perished in the flames. In the wake of this disaster, Malcolm X got up before a friendly audience and commented, with apparent glee: "I would like to announce a very beautiful thing"[2] and went on to tell about the crash. He summed up the disaster as being a message to him from Allah.

Despite this and other all-out verbal attacks on whites, he was still smarting from the Stokes incident. In early 1963 he called for a rally in Times Square in New York City to protest recent harassment by the police of local Muslim operations. Though advised by close associates to abandon the plan, he gathered several hundred Muslims for a march through the rush-hour crowds, creating an extremely explosive atmosphere. There were no incidents, but others around him at this time saw that he was frustrated enough to throw care to

Malcolm X addresses a rally at Harlem's Hotel Theresa in early 1963. The photo display is of the aftermath of the Stokes Incident.

the wind and to be unconcerned about anyone standing in his way.

Malcolm had already begun to feel tension between himself and the Nation. He had felt its resentment during the previous year, 1962, when his numerous speaking engagements and other activities on behalf of the Nation had received less and less coverage in the Nation's newspaper.[3] Now, in 1963, when major magazines like *Life* and *Newsweek* requested interviews with him, he turned them down; even though he knew the publicity would have been good for the organization, he felt that the Chicago-based Nation leadership opposed the publicity, and he dutifully assented to their viewpoint.[4]

Until the spring of 1963, Malcolm remained faithful to the Nation and especially to Elijah Muhammad. When doubts would enter his mind, he would refuse to consider them. He would castigate himself for even questioning any of the motives of the Nation, and he would double his efforts to think positively about the Nation and Elijah Muhammad.

During the spring of 1963, though, Malcolm's unswerving faith in Elijah Muhammad was tested. A few months earlier, in December 1962, several Muslims had publicly quit the organization, complaining of the improprieties of Elijah Muhammad himself. It was rumored that Elijah Muhammad had had affairs with several secretaries within the organization; he had even sired several children. Though these same rumors had touched Malcolm's ears back in 1955, he could no longer pretend to be deaf to them. He had to confront his mentor and find out the truth.

In April 1963, after the Stokes incident, Malcolm boarded a plane in New York and flew to Elijah Muhammad's palatial home in Phoenix, Arizona (the Nation had recently purchased it so the Messenger would have a place to go that would help his bouts with asthma). After greeting his young protege, the aging Prophet spoke of Biblical episodes of lust and of adultery; he then insisted he had to fulfill those things. Malcolm, stunned, took these pronouncements as an indication of guilt. It was as if Elijah Muhammad was arguing that Biblical personages had performed these deeds, so why shouldn't he? Malcolm boarded a plane and flew back to New York, certain his time with the Nation was running out.

But for the time being, he continued to speak and act in his capacity as Minister of Islam. That spring, as Martin Luther King, Jr., Bayard Rustin, Roy Wilkins, and other black leaders took center stage in the historic March on Washington, Malcolm dutifully called it the "Farce on Washington" and condemned the effort for not being a march for black people. Instead, he proclaimed it a march polluted by the effort of liberal whites. The march "ceased to be angry. It ceased to be impatient. In fact, it ceased to be a march. It became a picnic."[5]

King had always been a favorite target of Malcolm. In his regular speeches Malcolm would habitually include King's name with other names he said were handed down to the black slaves from their white slave masters—names including Smith, Jones, Bunche (as in Ralph Bunche, U.S. diplomat with the United Nations), and Wilkins (as in Roy Wilkins, director of the NAACP).

He could also be more direct with King, even when it meant he'd raise the ire of blacks outside the Nation of Islam. After viewing images from the 1963 Birmingham, Alabama, civil rights marches, during which black men, women, and children were pummeled by police and bitten by their dogs and sent flying across streets by the force of powerful firehoses, Malcolm X exclaimed: "Martin Luther King is a chump, not a champ. Any man who puts his women and children on the front lines is a chump, not a champ."

The response from the black community to these remarks was negative; Malcolm had attacked the feeling of unity that blacks all over the country felt watching those horrible images. Writer Louis Lomax asserts that if Martin Luther King was a chump, "so were we all."[6]

Malcolm would finally go too far with his personal attacks. One week after the November 22, 1963, assassination of President John F. Kennedy in Dallas,

84

Texas, Malcolm spoke at a Muslim rally in New York. While many might have felt that Malcolm would come up with something biting to say, he had been called earlier by Elijah Muhammad and told not to say anything about the assassination.

The audience heard nothing out of the ordinary for the entirety of the speech. He spoke about Kennedy's civil rights record and made some derogatory remarks on the recent March on Washington. But in a question and answer period after the speech, he loosened his lip. Asked to respond to the assassination, he said that it was a case of "the chickens coming home to roost." Further, he said "Being an old farm boy myself, chickens coming home to roost never did make me sad; they've always made me glad."[7] A big grin spread over his face.

The next morning, papers carried the words of Malcolm X, and people responded. Blacks and whites alike felt wounded, especially with the horrific day of the assassination so near in memory.

Malcolm was quickly summoned to Chicago and suspended for ninety days for speaking for the Nation of Islam. He had disobeyed Elijah Muhammad's order to keep quiet about the assassination, and his remarks had seriously damaged their image. He accepted the decision with grace and pledged his continuing allegiance to Elijah Muhammad.

Back in New York, it soon became apparent that being reinstated into the Nation of Islam was not just a matter of waiting out the ninety days. First, it was rumored that a replacement had already been appointed in Malcolm's place to head Temple Number Seven. Second, he thought he had been banned only from speaking to the press, but when he tried to step up to the podium at a temple meeting, he was prevented, by force, from doing so.

His emotional turmoil during these precarious weeks was great. To temple members, he sounded tired and tense. His confidence had been struck a blow. To reporters, there was a frailty about him they'd never seen before. He even asked for the dreaded white man's opinion on some things. He complained of headaches and stomach pains, though doctors found nothing wrong with him. One day, boxer Muhammad Ali, then Cassius Clay, telephoned from his Miami, Florida, training camp. The two had met a few years before and now Ali invited Malcolm and his family to come for a visit. Malcolm gratefully accepted.

In Miami, Malcolm tried to turn his attention from the events involving the Nation of Islam. He coached Clay, who had been a Muslim since 1962, on preparing for his boxing match with world champion Sonny Liston. He approved of Clay's strategy of trying to upset Liston with public name-calling and tantrums before the fight, to distract "the big ugly bear," as Clay called Liston, from his fight plan. He rejoiced as Clay defeated the angry and overconfident Liston in six rounds to

Malcolm shown with boxing champion Muhammad Ali. Says photographer Robert Haggins, ". . . you can call this one the 'Championship Tour.' This was a day or so after Ali won the title. He and Malcolm went on a walk down Harlem's 125th Street, shaking hands and meeting people, then they returned to the hotel."

become the world champion. He was proud the day after the fight when the boxer announced to the world press that he was a Muslim, and that his name was now Muhammad Ali.

Malcolm enjoyed the company of Ali, and in New York after the fight, Malcolm strolled around Harlem with the new heavyweight champ. But Malcolm could not really get the Nation of Islam out of his mind. He later told writer Alex Haley of his distracted state of mind in Miami: "I walked, I talked, I functioned."[8]

Back in New York, as Malcolm waited for the reinstatement deadline to come, he came to realize that the suspension was indeed permanent. Elijah Muhammad had expressed to the press that Malcolm X would be forgiven if he submitted—but hadn't he submitted already, in Chicago, right after the initial incident? Malcolm had petitioned Elijah Muhammad on several occasions during the suspension period—but why were all his requests to meet with Elijah Muhammad refused? And members in the Nation close to Malcolm had come to him with rumors of assassination orders handed down by other leaders.

On March 8, a week after the suspension was to have run out, he issued a momentous press release. That day, the *New York Times* ran this headline: "Malcolm X Splits With Muhammad." Two days later, on March 10, the Nation of Islam sent Malcolm a certified letter containing an eviction notice, notifying him that he was to move out of his East Elmhurst home immediately.

Malcolm's personal feelings for Elijah Muhammad were still strong. Well after the breakup, it was acknowledged among those close to Malcolm that if Elijah Muhammad would have made the first move toward real reconciliation, Malcolm would have gone back to him in a moment. Many scholars have pointed out how important Elijah Muhammad was as a sort of father-figure to Malcolm.

But either from hurt or anger, or from the sense of strategically fighting back to protect himself, Malcolm began to talk publicly of the negative things about Elijah Muhammad. He said that he himself had done many bad things in his life but had admitted his mistakes and worked in ways that made up for the transgressions. To Malcolm, Elijah Muhammad hadn't been quick to act regarding the scandal over the illegitimate children.

As he began thinking about his future, he perhaps began to feel as if a world were crumbling behind him as he stepped through an open door. The Nation of Islam had indeed lifted him out of self-degradation and had given him a sense of self-respect, but it had also reined him in with its religious and racial dogma. Now, he could entertain thoughts and ideas that he had gotten used to automatically shutting his eyes to. Now he could speak not for the honorable Elijah Muhammad, but for himself. Now, in the words of Peter Goldman, "The sun was up for Malcolm, flooding the darkness he had inhabited for more than a decade; and in its brilliant light, he could see his sanity, his only course of action and his death."[9]

Transformations

On March 9, 1964, the *New York Times* carried reports of Malcolm's new plans. The paper announced that among other things, he was prepared to form alliances with other black leaders and cooperate in local civil rights actions in the South and elsewhere. "I'm going to join in the fight wherever Negroes ask for my help," he said.[1]

The Malcolm that met reporters three days later at the Park Sheraton Hotel in New York was more confident and affable than reporters had recently seen. He announced to them the creation of Muslim Mosque, Incorporated, based on the principles of orthodox Islam. MMI would fight for economic and social concerns in black Muslim communities. Whites could provide ideas and money, but they could not join the organization.

"There can be no black-white unity until there is first some black unity . . ." he advised.[2]

Malcolm enchanted the media. He laughed with them as he enthusiastically answered their questions. He called them by their first names. Reporter Peter Goldman was at the Park Sheraton conference and remembers the surprise of one of the woman reporters from a local television station: "He's so—charming," exclaimed the reporter. "So intelligent."[3]

Some of his positions appeared to have softened, and Malcolm now made efforts to bring himself closer to the civil rights movement. But there seemed to be plenty of bad blood from the past remaining. He did not hear much from movement leaders, who might have also feared him as a competitor.

Regardless of the opinion of others, Malcolm was listening and learning from influences around him. He told a newspaperman that he was reading an awful lot now, to catch up with what he'd missed while in the Nation. As he had before in his life, he was again transforming himself.

Near the end of March, he met his long-time rival, Martin Luther King, Jr., for the first and only time. The two men encountered each other in a hallway in the U.S. Capitol building after a King news conference on March 26. They were friendly towards one another and photographers pushed and shoved to get pictures of the two men shaking hands.

Because of Malcolm's public attacks on King, people always pitted the men against one another, making each a representative of different ways to make change: peacefully or violently. Many thus think that the two men were enemies. In fact, each was concerned with what the other was thinking, and each greatly admired the other.

This observation is maintained by author Alex Haley, who, in early 1964, was working with Malcolm on his autobiography. Haley would travel to the South for an interview with King, who would casually ask, after an hour or so, what Malcolm was saying about him lately. Back in New York, Haley would be asked by Malcolm what King had said about him. "I'm convinced," wrote Haley, "that privately the two men felt mutual admiration and respect."[4]

Malcolm received trust and admiration from other people at this time as well. He had already met various representatives of African and Arab nations at the United Nations in New York and had been invited to their gatherings and affairs. The United Nations, he thought, might someday be an arena for the world's condemnation of America for its human rights violations against blacks.

To the Nation of Islam, though, Malcolm was the one who had committed a violation. Setting up a Muslim mosque outside the Nation of Islam was considered by the Nation to be a heresy. Shortly after the split, *Muhammad Speaks!*, the newspaper that Malcolm had started up years before, began denouncing him as a traitor. His older brother Philbert, still a leading minister in the organization, publicly condemned him. Elijah Muhammad expressed deep disappointment at his former minister's actions.

Malcolm tried not to display any ill will towards Elijah Muhammad. One reason for this might have been the practical strategy of trying not to excessively annoy one's enemies. At the same time he continued to feel grateful for the influence Elijah Muhammad had had on him personally.

He was also grateful for his most recent learning experience. At this time, he was getting more and more interested in Islam—traditional Islam, which was quite distinct from the Nation of Islam's doctrine. Several friends from the United Nations advised him to talk to Dr. Mahmoud Youssef Shawarbi, an Egyptian learned in Islam who directed the Islamic Center in New York City. Malcolm would sneak off downtown to Shawarbi's office, where the two men would discuss Islam. Actually, Shawarbi taught and Malcolm listened.

Malcolm's sessions with Dr. Shawarbi were momentous. At one point, learning the true meanings of traditional Islam's teaching brought Malcolm to tears. He was urged by Shawarbi to make the hajj, the pilgrimage to Mecca, in Saudi Arabia, that is required of every Muslim at least once in his life. Malcolm borrowed money from his half-sister Ella. Under the name of Malik El-Shabazz, he flew to Frankfurt, then on to Cairo and finally Saudi Arabia.

In Mecca, Malcolm beheld the birthplace of the prophet Muhammad, who had lived some thirteen centuries before. Malcolm was impressed with the calm and sense of power and stability of the ancient city.

He was also overwhelmed by the fact that everywhere he looked he saw men and women who had come from all corners of the world, united now in the holy city not by their skin color, but by their love of Islam. Surely he had seen light-skinned Muslims before, most probably on his first trip to Africa in 1959. But then he had in a sense worn blinders, keeping him from acknowledging that there were in fact light-skinned Muslims, a fact which flew in the face of Elijah Muhammad's teachings that all whites were devils.

Wearing sandals and wrapped in Ihram (two white cotton cloths), Malcolm carried out the necessary rituals required of all Muslims making their hajj. He circled seven times the large, black, boxlike shrine called the Kaaba, which held a black stone said to have been given to Adam when he fell from paradise. Malcolm ran seven times back and forth between the hills of Mt. Al-Safa and Al-Marwah and then drank from the holy well of Zem Zem. He recited special prayers in the ancient city of Mina and on Mt. Arafat. Within a few days he completed the hajj.

Mecca transformed Malcolm. He expressed his enthusiasm to the people he met and in his letters to friends in the United States. In a letter to James Farmer, former rival and now his friend, Malcolm said that he had just visited Mecca and "witnessed pilgrims of all colors, from every part of this earth, displaying a spirit of unity and brotherhood like I've never witnessed during my entire life in America. It is truly a wonderful sight to behold."[5] Many other friends and acquaintances received similar letters.

After Mecca, Malcolm happily toured other African countries. Everywhere he went, he found himself welcome. He discussed politics and spoke of his ideas for the future with government officials, at universities, and in the streets of the African cities and towns. "I feel that I am at home," he said in a speech at the University of Ghana. "I've been away for 400 years but not of my own volition, not of my own will."[6]

Just before Malcolm's return to the United States a curious incident occurred. On May 17, 1964, in the airport in Accra, Ghana's capital city, Malcolm encountered Muhammad Ali while walking through the terminal. Ali was also on a tour of Africa. The two men exchanged glances, then the heavyweight champ looked away from his former friend, now an enemy of the Nation of Islam. Malcolm appeared to be deeply upset by this incident.

Despite that hurt, though, Malcolm had had a

The great holy mosque in Mecca is Islam's shrine. The courtyard contains the large, black, boxlike shrine called the Kaaba, which holds a black stone said to have been given to Adam when he fell from paradise. Also within the courtyard is the holy well of Zem Zem.

gratifying journey. He arrived back in New York wearing a wispy beard and an African astrakhan hat. Looking fatigued but content, he fielded media questions.

Had any of his views changed since the visit? Well, for one thing, intermarriage was no longer an issue. "It's just one human being marrying another human being, or one human being living around and with another human being."[7] He was also no longer concerned with creating a separate black state.

And did he have anything new to say about his feelings for whites? Well, he had done a lot of thinking on that. He announced to the media that he no longer felt that whites were devils. He now believed in what Islam's holy book, the Koran, teaches: that a man shouldn't be judged by skin color but by "his conscious behavior, by his actions, by his attitude towards others and his actions toward others."[8] It was a striking shift from his prior thinking. But to him it was truth, and he couldn't deny it.

A little over a month after his return, on June 28, 1964, the "new" Malcolm announced the formation of the Organization of Afro-American Unity. The OAAU would work to define Harlem as more of an African state than an American city. It would try to get people all over the world to see that Harlem's problems were not New York's or America's problems—they were African problems. Injustices against American blacks would no longer be civil rights issues—they would become human

Friday 9 AM – April 25, 1964

Dear Alex Haley:

I have just completed my pilgrimage
(Hajj) to the Holy City of Mecca, the Holiest
City in Islam, which is absolutely forbidden
for non-believers even to rest their eyes
upon. There were over 200,000 pilgrims
there, at the same time. This pilgrimage
is to the Muslim, as important as is going
to "heaven" to the Christian. I doubt if there
have been more ~~than~~ than ten Americans to
ever make this pilgrimage. I know of
only two others who have actually made the
Hajj (and both of them are West Indian). Mr
Muhammad and two of his sons made what
is known as "Omra" (the pilgrimage or "visit"
to Mecca outside of the Hajj season). I think
I'm the first American born Negro to make
the actual Hajj --- and if I'm not the

The first page of a letter from Malcolm X to Alex Haley,
dated Friday, April 25, 1964. The stationary is from a
hotel in Jedda, Saudi Arabia, about fifty miles from the
holy city of Mecca.

rights issues. They would be argued not in the Supreme Court but at the United Nations.

To gain African support for his new organization, he appeared in Cairo on July 17 at the African Summit Conference, which was attended by representatives of most of the nations of Africa. On that day he appealed to the other delegates to think about joining together at the United Nations to speak as one voice in opposition to the treatment of the 22 million blacks in the United States. The response was promising. He returned to Africa again in September, traveling from country to country as a guest of the heads of various states. He busily addressed parliaments, informed high officials of the problems in America, and grew acquainted with the problems in his host countries.

Back again in New York, despite the joy he felt at the birth of his fourth daughter, Gamilah, Malcolm felt that his time was running out. The Nation wanted him out of his East Elmhurst house, and they were infuriated with him for things he was saying about Elijah Muhammad. To any reporter who asked, Malcolm had been backing up the story that Muhammad had sired children by his secretaries. When one reporter privately expressed his concern that Malcolm might be in danger for publicly saying such things, Malcolm responded, "Yes, I'm probably a dead man already."[9]

To Alex Haley, his biographer, he would say vaguely that the things that were happening in his life lately weren't being done by the Nation of Islam. Something must have made him believe that some larger organization, perhaps the U.S. government itself, was hunting him down. Whenever he climbed into his blue Oldsmobile with a friend or reporter, he'd snap his fingers several times and say "testing, one two, one two," as if speaking to a hidden microphone.

With this sense of time running out, he pushed forward, speaking to new audiences here and abroad, all the time listening and reexamining his views. But while he was changing, others weren't keeping up with him. His old images of "Black Muslim" and "hatemonger" were hard to shake and kept some of the more moderate civil rights organizations from working with him. Yet black militants avoided him as being too moderate. He told author Alex Haley in early January, 1965, "They won't let me turn the corner . . . I'm caught in a trap!"[10]

He did turn a corner on February 4, 1965, though. On that day, at the request of the Student Nonviolent Coordinating Committee (SNCC) which had staged successful sit-ins in the South, Malcolm traveled down to Selma, Alabama.

In Selma he addressed a rally for voting rights, which were then not ensured for all black citizens of Alabama. On this day, Martin Luther King, Jr., was in jail. His wife Coretta was seated onstage with other black leaders, who feared Malcolm might incite the crowd to violence. But Malcolm's words merely warned; they did not

A tense and weary Malcolm X sat for this photograph in early 1965.

provoke. He told the audience that if whites knew what the alternative was, they would probably be more apt to listen to Dr. King.[11] With this appearance, black leaders grew hopeful for an alliance between Malcolm and themselves, including Dr. King himself.

Malcolm continued his strenuous travel schedule. The very next day, February 5, he again flew to England; in London he addressed the First Congress of the Council of African Organizations. Afterwards he flew to Paris but he was denied entry for no clear reason. Disturbed by this turn of events, he returned to the United States—this time for good.

Life became more and more dangerous. After a speaking engagement in Boston, an unidentified car followed a car that Malcolm was thought to be in, but which actually contained other members of Malcolm's entourage. There was a confrontation, but the men from the other car were scared off by the sight of a shotgun. In Chicago, he was almost ambushed by two cars that pulled alongside his car, racing to the airport. Thinking quickly, Malcolm rolled down his window and stuck out a walking cane. In the dark the cane looked like a rifle, and the other cars fell back and disappeared.

Malcolm did what he could to help and protect his family. The flow of money sent to him regularly by the Nation of Islam had been shut off after he left the movement, and now he accepted speaking engagements wherever and whenever he could. He told Alex Haley to funnel any profits from the publication of his upcoming autobiography to his family and not to Elijah Muhammad's Nation. He gave Betty a shotgun to use in case anyone tried to get in their house in East Elmhurst.

Fears for the safety of his family materialized in the early morning hours of February 14. One moment the night was calm and quiet, the next moment there was the sound of breaking glass and an explosion, and the East Elmhurst house was ablaze.

Betty Shabazz remembers the night their home was firebombed: "I went into such shock. I was actually immobilized. But Malcolm was cool, sure, and swift. He found me at the kitchen door, to let the smoke out and told me to stay there. Then he brought the children to me. That loosened me up and brought me back to life. He ran back into the house for some of our belongings. I was almost frightened by his courage and efficiency in a time of terror. I always knew he was strong, but at that hour I learned how great his strength was."[12]

It was terribly hard to remain strong, though. Malcolm seemed resigned to what he saw as his impending death. He refused to accept an invitation to sleep at an associate's house for fear of endangering other people. His nerves were frayed; he lost his temper with others. He spoke to author Alex Haley the night of February 20 and asked, in a tired, stressed voice, if Haley would help him get some money together to buy a new house. That was the last time Haley heard Malcolm's voice.

The next day, February 21, Malcolm was scheduled to speak at the Audubon Ballroom in Harlem. Benjamin Karim came onto the stage to deliver the introduction. Karim recalled the tension in the air. "I felt like a big gorilla was sitting on my shoulders. I believe I felt the same thing he did . . . I felt it. And I watched him."[13]

Malcolm strode to the microphone to address the audience. He leaned toward the microphone, grinned to the audience, received their applause. "As-salaam alaikum," he said. "Peace, peace." Those were his last words.

Suddenly two men near the back stood and began arguing with one another. The crowd turned to watch. Security guards left their posts. All were distracted by the altercation—even Malcolm himself, who may or may not have seen three men in the first few rows rise and push away their overcoats to reveal their weapons, which they leveled and aimed. Sixteen shotgun slugs and revolver bullets tore into Malcolm. He fell backwards. The room erupted in terrified screams and shouts and cries. Someone threw a smokebomb. People scrambled for the front door exits.

Malcolm's photographer, Robert Haggins, was just approaching the Audubon when Malcolm was shot. "It's built like a ballroom, for music, so sound does not travel to the street . . . what we saw first, from outside, was a

Malcolm X being wheeled out of the Audubon Ballroom the day of his assassination. Photographer Robert Haggins arrived right after Malcolm was shot: "...they brought Malcolm out on a stretcher. He went right past me. I could see that he was dead."

man running down the steps, bleeding from the leg. This was one of the assassins. People behind him started yelling 'stop him, stop him.' Somebody asked why, and somebody replied. 'He shot Malcolm.' Then the crowd closed on him. I saw his head being kicked around like a football. The police arrived and pulled him out of there. They then brought Malcolm out on a stretcher. He went right past me. I could see that he was dead."[14]

Things Change, Things Remain the Same

For many people, the news of the assassination generated rage. Eldridge Cleaver, devout Muslim and member of the Black Panthers, a militant black organization, was serving a sentence at Folsom Prison in California when Malcolm X was assassinated. In his book *Soul On Ice*, Cleaver recalls that a violence raged up in him and other Black Muslims in the prison: "What does one say to his comrades at the moment when The Leader falls: All comment seems irrelevant. If the source of death is so-called natural causes, or an accident, the reaction is predictable, a feeling of impotence, humbleness, helplessness before the forces of the universe.

"But when the cause of death is an assassin's bullet, the overpowering desire is for vengeance. One wants to strike out, to kill, crush, destroy, to deliver a telling counterblow, to inflict upon the enemy a reciprocal, equivalent loss."[1]

Rage bubbled over in the streets of Harlem, and a counterblow was inflicted. Though Elijah Muhammad had immediately denied that he was responsible for the shooting, the day after the assassination, Harlem Mosque Number Seven was burned almost to the ground. After firefighters put out the blaze, people wandered by in the February cold, eyeing the smoldering remains and the ice-like prison bars in the burned-out windows, remembering when Malcolm proudly held court there.

Rage was not the only response to Malcolm's assassination. Many newspapers responded with apparent satisfaction to his death. The *New York Times* announced: "The Apostle of Hate is Dead."[2] It was as if he had gotten what he always deserved, as if in dying by the sword he had lived by the sword. They were glad to be rid of his troublesome voice at last.

But there were many who felt a great sadness, a great sense of loss. This was evident especially among the people of Harlem. About 22,000 people stood in line and glimpsed him in the Faith Temple Church of God in Christ on Amsterdam Avenue in Harlem for the last time, as he lay in his open-faced bronze coffin. The people of Harlem came to say goodbye, paying their last respects under the eyes of plainclothes police and Malcolm's armed supporters. Bomb threats closed off the church now and again.

The eulogy was given by actor and activist Ossie Davis, a longtime friend of Malcolm's. Davis spoke to the mourners about how Malcolm was a hero to black people. He told them about how in honoring Malcolm, blacks honored what was best in themselves. He spoke of Malcolm as "our manhood, our living, black manhood!" And he concluded his stirring speech with the insistence that Malcolm was "a Prince—our own black shining Prince!—who didn't hesitate to die, because he loved us so."[3] Malcolm's coffin was taken out of the city, to rural Hartsdale, New York, and buried in Ferncliff Cemetery.

Three Muslims charged with the assassination of Malcolm X awaited trial. Talmadge Hayer, Norman 3X Butler, and Thomas 15X Johnson had been arrested at the Audubon Ballroom right after the assassination. In March of the following year, 1966, they were convicted of first-degree murder in connection with Malcolm's death and sentenced to life imprisonment.

People have since claimed that there was a conspiracy to kill Malcolm X. Many believe that despite Elijah Muhammad's denials, the Nation of Islam orchestrated Malcolm's assassination. Some claim that the FBI and the CIA were involved, too, and perhaps even the New York Police Department. Malcolm himself and those close to him believed there were strong, organized forces out to kill him.

While Malcolm had plenty of enemies, and while it is known that the FBI began spying on him in 1953, evidence for the conspiracy theories is questionable. Michael Friedly, author of *Malcolm X: The Assassination,* claims that the best evidence available suggests that Malcolm's assassination was planned by five members—three gunmen and the two who acted as a distraction—of the Newark Mosque, on their own, with no one else's knowledge or assistance. Talmadge Hayer was a triggerman, but the other two originally convicted with him were innocent. In 1979, Hayer finally revealed the names and addresses of the four other alleged assassins of Malcolm X. All were members of the Newark, New Jersey, Mosque. But no new trial was approved by New York State and the four men were never pursued. Friedly reports that Hayer, Butler, and Johnson were paroled in the mid-eighties and live today in obscurity.[4]

Rage like the rage that erupted in the wake of Malcolm's assassination in 1965 simmered and sometimes boiled throughout the decade. In the year before Malcolm's assassination, riots had broken out in New York, New Jersey, Chicago, and Philadelphia; one year after his death, South Central Los Angeles burned. Poor urban blacks saw no improvement in their lives due to the civil rights movement; they still lived in poverty, fear, and hopelessness.

There was also some progress in that turbulent

decade, though. Among many "firsts" for blacks, Thurgood Marshall became the first black justice on the Supreme Court. Martin Luther King, Jr.'s popularity and influence grew. White political leaders like Robert Kennedy fought for civil rights. A militant organization called the Black Panthers insisted upon black pride and self-defense, and they carried weapons. They had the support of revolutionaries around the world, including that of leaders from the many African nations that had only recently freed themselves from the white governments that had ruled them. There was hope for real change in the living conditions of blacks in America.

But all too often, hope died in violence. King was assassinated. Kennedy, on the verge of becoming the Democratic candidate for the presidency, was also assassinated. By the end of the decade members of the Black Panthers were hounded into silence, jailed, or killed.

In the decades that have followed, while blacks continued to make political advances—by 1984 black mayors had been elected in over 250 cities around the country—living conditions for urban blacks have not improved. Since 1967, the proportion of black families living at the lowest income level, according to the Census Bureau, grew by fifty percent.[5]

Frustration and rage have continued on into the 1990s. In early 1992, South Central Los Angeles went up in flames, as it had almost thirty years before. This time the spark was the acquittal of white police officers in the beating of a black man, Rodney King. The King beating and the circumstances surrounding it reminded many of the death of Ronald Stokes at the hands of white police officers in 1962 and the subsequent dropping of the charges against the policemen. Malcolm would have seen the similarity.

What if Malcolm X had lived? Author Bruce Perry suggests that he might very well have run for then-Congressman Adam Clayton Powell's Harlem seat and won it. He might have been New York City's first black mayor. "He certainly was smart enough," says Perry.[6] He may have even run for president. It is true that at the end of his short life, he had not been good at working with others and compromising, as is necessary in politics, but he might have learned to do this. Why not? He had always been able to change.

In recent years, though, it has been the *story* of Malcolm X that has gone through changes. *The Autobiography of Malcolm X* (as told to Alex Haley) was published just a few months after Malcolm's death. The work was a moving account of the various phases in his life, according to Malcolm. It met with terrific success. It went through eighteen printings in less than five years and became required reading in schools and colleges all over the country. In 1992, a long-awaited movie about Malcolm X, directed by Spike Lee, was an immediate hit at the box office.

The film, which grossed nearly $45 million in the two months following its release, was also based on the events reported in the autobiography.[7]

However, scholars recently have begun to question certain events in the work. For instance, Malcolm, in the *Autobiography*, asserted that before he was born, white terrorists set fire to the family house in Omaha, Nebraska; that the torching of the Little home in Lansing years later when he was a child was also the work of white terrorists; and that Earl Little was beaten and pushed under a trolley by the same white hate group. These assertions have since been strongly questioned. Other portrayals of Malcolm's life, in the *Autobiography*, like his friendship with famous musicians in Harlem and his stature as a criminal there, appear to have been exaggerated.

Who was Malcolm X? We will probably understand much more about him as scholars continue their work of digging into his early life. But the facts of his life may always take a back seat to who people think he was, and what quality they find in him to relate to, whether it is rage, pride, discipline, courage, or humanity. "Everybody has their own Malcolm," says filmmaker Spike Lee.[8]

Who was Malcolm X? One quality that he consistently showed in his life was his ability to change: to listen, to accept that he was wrong, to learn, and to grow. And ultimately to transform himself. Poet Maya

Malcolm X at home with his wife, Betty, and two of his daughters.

Angelou remembers Malcolm's transformation during his trip to Mecca: ". . . most people would rather like to say what they say they believe in and then repeat themselves instead of saying, 'I'm not in love with the position, I'm in love with the search for truth'—and that was Malcolm."[9]

Chronology

1925— Malcolm Little is born on May 19 at University Hospital in Omaha, Nebraska.

1931— Earl Little is run over by a streetcar and killed.

1939— Louise Little is declared legally insane and moved to the State Mental Hospital in Kalamazoo, Michigan.

1940— Malcolm goes to live with his half-sister, Ella Collins, in Boston, Massachusetts.

1943— Malcolm moves to Harlem, New York City.

1946— Malcolm is sent to jail in Massachusetts on charges of robbery.

1947— Malcolm converts to the teachings of Elijah Muhammad and the Nation of Islam.

1952— Following his release from prison, Malcolm meets Elijah Muhammad in Chicago while staying with family in Detroit; begins working for the Nation of Islam and receives his "X."

1957— Malcolm and members of Temple Number Seven come to the aid of fellow member Johnson Hinton, beaten and detained by police.

1958— In January, Malcolm marries Betty X; in November their first child, Attilah, is born.

1960— Malcolm and Betty's second daughter, Qubilah, is born.

1962— Malcolm and Betty's third daughter, Ilyasah, is born.

1963— Malcolm is suspended from his ministry by Elijah Muhammad.

1964— Malcolm breaks with the Nation of Islam, forms Muslim Mosque, Inc., and the OAAU, and makes a pilgrimage to Mecca. Gamilah, a fourth daughter, is born to Malcolm and Betty.

1965— On February 14, Malcolm's house in East Elmhurst is firebombed; on February 21, Malcolm is shot to death at the Audubon Ballroom in Harlem; that summer, Betty Shabazz gives birth to twin daughters, Malaak and Malikah.

Chapter Notes

Chapter 1

1. Robert Penn Warren, "Who Speaks For The Negro?" in David Gallen, *Malcolm X: As They Knew Him* (New York: Carroll and Graf Publishers, Inc., 1992), p. 204.

2. Alex Haley and Malcolm X, *The Autobiography of Malcolm X* (New York: Ballantine Books, 1992), p. 233.

3. Ibid., p. 234.

4. Ibid.

5. Ibid.

6. Ibid.

7. Mark Davies, *Malcolm X: Another Side of the Movement* (Englewood Cliffs, N.J.: Silver Burdett Press, 1990).

8. Alex Haley and Malcolm X, p. 235.

Chapter 2

1. "The Playboy Interview: Malcolm X Speaks with Alex Haley," in David Gallen, *Malcolm X: As They Knew Him* (New York: Carroll and Graf Publishers, Inc., 1992), p. 122.

2. Bruce Perry, *Malcolm: The Life of a Man Who Changed Black America* (Barrytown, N.Y.: Station Hill Press, Inc., 1991), pp. 6, 8.

3. Ibid., p. 3.

4. Ibid., p. 5.

5. Alex Haley and Malcolm X, *The Autobiography of Malcolm X* (New York: Ballantine Books, 1992), p. 7.

6. Bruce Perry, p. 12.

7. Ibid., p. 15.

8. Ibid., p. 15.

9. Ibid., p. 33.

10. Ibid., p. 38.

11. Ibid., p. 39.

12. Ibid., p. 42.

13. Ibid.

14. Richard Curtis, *The Life of Malcolm X* (Philadelphia: Macrae Smith Company, 1971), p. 27.

Chapter 3

1. Roi Ottley, *New World A-Coming: Inside Black America* (Boston: Houghton Mifflin Company, 1943), p. 1.

2. Ibid.

3. Alex Haley and Malcolm X, *The Autobiography of Malcolm X* (New York: Ballantine Books, 1992), p. 75.

4. Ibid., p. 91.

5. Ibid., p. 106.

6. "The Playboy Interview: Malcolm X Speaks with Alex Haley," in David Gallen, *Malcolm X: As They Knew Him* (New York: Carroll and Graf Publishers, Inc., 1992), p. 123.

7. Alex Haley and Malcolm X, p. 149.

8. Peter Goldman, *The Death and Life of Malcolm X*, 2nd. ed. (Chicago: University of Illinois Press, 1979), p. 33.

Chapter 4

1. Peter Goldman, *The Death and Life of Malcolm X*, 2nd. ed. (Chicago: University of Illinois Press, 1979), p. 154.

2. Bruce Perry, *Malcolm: The Life of a Man Who Changed Black America* (Barrytown, N.Y.: Station Hill Press, Inc., 1991), p. 108.

3. "The Playboy Interview: Malcolm X Speaks with Alex Haley," in David Gallen, *Malcolm X: As They Knew Him* (New York: Carroll and Graf Publishers, Inc., 1992), p. 119.

4. Henry Louis Gates, Jr., "Just Whose 'Malcolm' Is It, Anyway?: An Interview with Spike Lee," *New York Times* (May 31, 1992), Arts and Leisure, p. 13.

5. Bruce Perry, p. 113.

6. Information on the origins and theology of the Nation of Islam is based primarily on two sources: Peter Goldman, *The Death and Life of Malcolm X,* 2nd. ed. (Chicago: University of Illinois Press, 1979), pp. 35–43; and Malu Halasa, *Elijah Muhammad* (New York: Chelsea House Publishers, 1990), pp. 43–51.

7. Malu Halasa, p. 45.

8. Peter Goldman, p. 33.

9. Ibid., p. 33.

10. Ibid., p. 41.

11. Ibid., p. 84.

12. Robert Vernon, "Malcolm X: Voice of the Black Ghetto," *International Socialist Review* (Spring, 1965); in George Breitman, *The Last Year of Malcolm X* (New York: Pathfinder Press, 1989), p. 7.

13. Peter Goldman, p. 34.

14. George Breitman, p. 8.

15. Peter Goldman, p. 46.

Chapter 5

1. Peter Goldman, *The Death and Life of Malcolm X,* 2nd. ed. (Chicago: University of Illinois Press, 1979), p. 45.

2. Malu Halasa, *Elijah Muhammad* (New York: Chelsea House Publishers, 1990), p. 86.

3. Ibid., p. 76.

4. Ibid.

5. John Henrik Clarke, ed. *Malcolm X: The Man and His Times* (Trenton, N.J.: Arica World Press, Inc., 1990), p. 271.

6. Bruce Perry, *Malcolm: The Life of a Man Who Changed Black America* (Barrytown, N.Y.: Station Hill Press, Inc., 1991), p. 146.

7. Malu Halasa, p. 77.

8. Clayborne Carson, *Malcolm X: The FBI File* (New York: Carroll and Graf Publishers, Inc., 1991), p. 101.

9. Alex Haley and Malcolm X, *The Autobiography of Malcolm X* (New York: Ballantine Books, 1992), pp. 200–201.

10. Louis E. Lomax, *When the Word Is Given . . .* (Westport, Conn.: Greenwood Press, Publishers, 1963), p. 51.

11. Clayborne Carson, p. 120.

12. Bruce Perry, pp. 176–177.

13. Clayborne Carson, p. 117.

14. Alex Haley and Malcolm X, p. 210.

15. Ibid., p. 214.

16. Louis E. Lomax, p. 131.

17. Ibid., p. 97.

18. Peter Goldman, p. 67.

19. The recollection of the meeting and exchanges between Haggins and Malcolm X is from author's personal interview with Robert Haggins, September 9, 1992.

20. Malu Halasa, pp. 76–77.

21. Ibid., p. 84.

22. John Henrik Clarke, p. 271.

Chapter 6

1. Malu Halasa, *Elijah Muhammad* (New York: Chelsea House Publishers, 1990), p. 80.

2. Alex Haley, "Alex Haley Remembers," in David Gallen, *Malcolm X: As They Knew Him* (New York: Carroll and Graf Publishers, Inc., 1992), p. 247.

3. Clayborne Carson, *Malcolm X: The FBI File* (New York: Carroll and Graf Publishers, Inc., 1991), p. 179.

4. Peter Goldman, *The Death and Life of Malcolm X*, 2nd. ed. (Chicago: University of Illinois Press, 1979), p. 64.

5. Personal interview with Robert Haggins, September 9, 1992.

6. Bruce Perry, *Malcolm X: The Life of a Man Who Changed Black America* (Barrytown, N.Y.: Station Hill Press, Inc., 1991), p. 175.

7. Ibid., p. 197.

8. Peter Goldman, p. 63.

9. Bruce Perry, p. 178.

10. Ibid., p. 177.

11. Ibid., p. 178.

12. Clayborne Carson, p. 180.

13. Ibid., p. 183.

14. Louis E. Lomax, *When the Word Is Given . . .* (Westport, Conn.: Greenwood Press, Publishers, 1963), p. 129.

15. Bruce Perry, p. 214.

16. David Gallen and Peter Skutches, "As They Knew Him: Oral Remembrances of Malcolm X," in *Malcolm X: As They Knew Him* (New York: Carroll and Graf Publishers, Inc., 1992), p. 37.

17. Bruce Perry, p. 180.

Chapter 7

1. "The Ronald Stokes Incident: Brother Malcolm on WBAI with Richard Elman," in David Gallen, *Malcolm X: As They Knew Him* (New York: Carroll and Graf Publishers, Inc., 1992), p. 106.

2. Bruce Perry, *Malcolm: The Life of a Man Who Changed Black America* (Barrytown, N.Y.: Station Hill Press, Inc., 1991), p. 207.

3. Alex Haley and Malcolm X, *The Autobiography of Malcolm X* (New York: Ballantine Books, 1992), p. 292.

4. Ibid., p. 293.

5. Bruce Perry, p. 211.

6. Louis E. Lomax, *When the Word Is Given . . .* (Westport, Conn.: Greenwood Press, Publishers, 1963), p. 74.

7. Peter Goldman, *The Death and Life of Malcolm X*, 2nd. ed. (Chicago: University of Illinois Press, 1979), p. 118.

8. Bruce Perry, p. 246.

9. Peter Goldman, p. 132.

Chapter 8

1. George Breitman, *The Last Year of Malcolm X* (New York: Pathfinder Press, 1989), p. 20.

2. Peter Goldman, *The Death and Life of Malcolm X*, 2nd. ed. (Chicago: University of Illinois Press, 1979), p. 134.

3. Ibid., p. 136.

4. Alex Haley, "Alex Haley Remembers," in David Gallen, *Malcolm X: As They Knew Him* (New York: Carroll and Graf Publishers, Inc., 1992), p. 248.

5. Peter Goldman, p. 168.

6. Ibid., p. 176.

7. George Breitman, ed., *Malcolm X Speaks* (New York: Grove Weidenfeld, 1965), p. 197.

8. Pierre Berton, "Whatever is Necessary: The Last Television Interview, with Pierre Berton," in David Gallen, *Malcolm X: As They Knew Him* (New York: Carroll and Graf Publishers, Inc., 1992), p. 186.

9. David Gallen and Peter Skutches, "As They Knew Him: Oral Remembrances of Malcolm X," in *Malcolm X: As They Knew Him* (New York: Carroll and Graf Publishers, Inc., 1992), p. 86.

10. George Breitman, p. 26.

11. Juan Williams, *Eyes on the Prize* (New York: Penguin Books, 1988), p. 262.

12. Fletcher Knebel, "A Visit with the Widow of Malcolm X," *Look* magazine (March 4, 1969).

13. David Gallen and Peter Skutches, p. 93.

14. Personal interview with Robert Haggins, September 9, 1992.

Chapter 9

1. Eldridge Cleaver, *Soul On Ice* (New York: Dell Publishing Company, Inc., 1968), p. 51.

2. Peter Goldman, *The Death and Life of Malcolm X*, 2nd. ed. (Chicago: University of Illinois Press, 1979), p. 302.

3. Eldridge Cleaver, p. 200.

4. Telephone interview with Michael Friedly, October 29, 1992.

5. Felicia R. Lee, "Malcolm X, in the Eyes of Different Beholders," *New York Times* (November 1, 1992), Week in Review, p. 6.

6. Telephone interview with Bruce Perry, October 24, 1992.

7. *Entertainment, Inc.*, January 1993.

8. Henry Louis Gates, Jr., "Just Whose 'Malcolm' Is It, Anyway?: An Interview with Spike Lee," *New York Times* (May 31, 1992), Arts and Leisure, p. 13.

9. David Gallen and Peter Skutches, "As They Knew Him: Oral Remembrances of Malcolm X," in *Malcolm X: As They Knew Him* (New York: Carroll and Graf Publishers, Inc., 1992), p. 74.

Further Reading

Curtis, Richard. *The Life of Malcolm X.* Philadelphia: Macrae Smith Company, 1971.

Davies, Mark. *Malcolm X: Another Side of the Movement.* Englewood Cliffs, N.J.: Silver Burdett Press, 1990.

Goldman, Peter. *The Death and Life of Malcolm X.* 2nd. ed. Chicago: University of Illinois Press, 1979.

Halasa, Malu. *Elijah Muhammad.* New York: Chelsea House Publishers, 1990.

Haley, Alex and Malcolm X. *The Autobiography of Malcolm X.* New York: Ballantine Books, 1992.

Perry, Bruce. *Malcolm: The Life of a Man Who Changed Black America.* Barrytown, N.Y.: Station Hill Press, Inc., 1991.

Index

127